NARRATIVE CHANGE

Hans Hansen

NARRATIVE CHANGE

How Changing the Story
Can Transform Society,
Business, and Ourselves

Columbia University Press | New York

Columbia Business School
Publishing

Columbia University Press
Publishers Since 1893
New York   Chichester, West Sussex
cup.columbia.edu

Copyright © 2020 Columbia University Press
All rights reserved

Library of Congress Cataloging-in-Publication Data
Names: Hansen, Hans (College teacher), author.
Title: Narrative change : how changing the story can transform
    society, business, and ourselves / Hans Hansen.
Description: New York : Columbia University Press, [2020] |
    Includes bibliographical references and index.
Identifiers: LCCN 2019051925 (print) | LCCN 2019051926 (ebook) |
    ISBN 9780231184427 (hardback) | ISBN 9780231545488 (ebook)
Subjects: LCSH: Narrative inquiry (Research method) |
    Capital punishment—Texas. | Social change.
Classification: LCC H61.295 .H37 2020 (print) | LCC H61.295 (ebook) |
    DDC 364.6609764—dc23
LC record available at https://lccn.loc.gov/2019051925
LC ebook record available at https://lccn.loc.gov/2019051926

Columbia University Press books are printed on
permanent and durable acid-free paper.

Printed in the United States of America

Cover design: Lisa Hamm
Cover image: © lukbar/Adobe Stock

Contents

Acknowledgments   *vii*
Preface   *ix*

Introduction   1

1   No Place to Hide   12

2   Talking Narratives   18

3   How the Change Model Emerged   42

4   Applying the Model   55

5   The Narrative Stranglehold   72

6   Enacting New Narratives   94

7   Narrative Selection Versus Narrative Construction   109

8   Narratives as a Way to Organize   128

9   A Narrative for You   145

10   Big Ideas and Narrative Modes   159

Conclusion   *173*
Notes   *191*
References   *195*
Index   *199*

Acknowledgments

I would like to thank the Texas Regional Public Defender Office for Capital Cases for inviting me to work with them in fighting the death penalty, and for allowing me to conduct ethnographic research on their work and lives. I am particularly grateful to Philip Wischkaemper and Jack Stoffregen for giving me unprecedented access to a remarkable setting and for their willingness to try innovative approaches to stop executions. I also want to congratulate them on their tremendous success in changing the way the death penalty works in Texas. I am grateful to my family and my colleagues for supporting my work. I am also thankful for the guidance of my editor, Myles Thompson, at Columbia University Press.

Preface

This book offers a model of change for everyone, but it emerged from an unlikely tale of a small group of people who managed to change the way the death penalty operates in Texas. I have since tried, tested, and refined the model and applied it in a variety of settings. I am now confident enough to release it so others can benefit from what I have learned about the processes of change.

On one hand, this book came out of the blue. Changing the death penalty, a Goliath of an institution, began with an unexpected phone call from a lawyer wanting me to help build a small team of people. He was vague on the phone, and I agreed to meet with him, but only to get some more details about this new team and suggest someone more suitable than me to help them.

On the other hand, this book has been in the making for more than twenty years. I can see how all of my past experiences, even my shortcomings—maybe especially my shortcomings—prepared me for the challenge I faced in fighting the death penalty. Planned or unplanned, all of my experiences forged in me a perspective of change that would become invaluable.

Our tremendous success was unlikely. No one, not even the death penalty team members, ever imagined we would accomplish what we did. The team has stopped well over one hundred executions against nearly insurmountable odds. During my time with the team, we were 70 and 1, and now the team is 165 and 4.

This story begins in West Texas, where the powerful state got death sentences in capital trials more than 90 percent of the time. I learned a lot in working to change an extremely ingrained institution, and I think the same processes and model I used could work for any team, organization, or individual.

I knew I had to share it.

■ ■ ■

Recently, I had the opportunity to spend some time with someone I had long admired, Sister Helen Prejean. Sister Helen is the famous Catholic nun who wrote *Dead Man Walking*, which described her relationship with a death row inmate and her witness to the effects of the death penalty on everyone involved. Susan Sarandon played Sister Helen in the critically acclaimed movie of the same name and won an Academy Award.

Sister Helen and I shared our joys and struggles in wrestling with the death penalty, both of us having gone from unwitting outsiders to central players. I was so happy to finally meet someone whose introduction to the death penalty reflected my own. Neither Sister Helen nor I ever had any intention of getting involved with death penalty cases. In her case, someone casually suggested she write to a man in prison.

"I thought I was getting some sort of pen pal!" Sister Helen told me.

My introduction was that unexpected phone call requesting a meeting with a couple of lawyers who wanted advice on team building.

I am an ethnographer, which means I am a professional outsider-cum-insider. Learning how the death penalty works in practice was eye-opening and jaw-dropping. Attempting to fight it, much less stop it, seemed impossible. The death penalty is a brutal, unrelenting beast, and I felt like a bewildered nincompoop who had accidently wandered into the ring with a monster.

Mirroring my own feelings, Sister Helen told me one of her favorite stories about her own lack of readiness involving a movie production meeting with director Tim Robbins and Susan Sarandon. They were discussing characterization for various movie roles when Tim surmised: "Clearly, the nun is in over her head."

"And I was!" Sister Helen laughed.

It was cathartic for me to hear that Sister Helen and I shared so many of the same emotions in our respective journeys. I too felt ill equipped and unprepared for what lay ahead once I agreed to help the death penalty defense team change the way they did things. "If this is fate," I once told a crowd, "she could not have picked worse."

I did not want to get involved—in anything. I had made a pretty conscious decision to hide from the world, not fight one of its most menacing demons. But something pulled me in, or maybe I jumped. I like to think I yearned to make a difference, but maybe I knew it might just save my life.

In the early days, I kept asking, "What if we try this?" while spit-balling strategies to fight the death penalty.

Experienced experts kept saying, "It's never been done, but let's try it."

It was nerve-racking. Even though I was confident, it never escaped me that lives were on the line. I shared my fears by reminding the team, constantly, that I was only there by mistake.

"Or luck," someone said.

Either way, I felt like I did not belong. Over time, I grew into the task, and we were enormously successful. Death penalty defense has changed. So have I. My broader ideas about managing and leading change have been tested and refined, and now I want to share them with you. If you face a change challenge, whether you have sought it or it has fallen to you, I think you will find the ideas in this book useful.

No matter the size of the job, or how intractable the problems may seem, you can change the ways thing are.

■ ■ ■

Out of respect for the families of the victims, names and other identifying details in several of the cases have been changed.

NARRATIVE CHANGE

Introduction

This book is about leading change by creating and enacting new narratives. The simplest and broadest conceptualization of change is moving from the old way of doing things to a new way of doing things. Although this is easily said, making these changes entails understanding many subtle processes that we rarely examine. To lead transformational change, we need to devote attention to two main processes. The first—the most overlooked aspect of change in both our theories and practices—is overcoming or resisting pressures to keep doing things the same way we have "always" done things. The second is enacting change, bringing new ideas and vision into the real world. My method calls for creating and enacting narratives.

Narratives are central to change and overlap conceptually with change. Almost all change models describe several stages, beginning with a current state, describing actions that move or change things, and establishing a new future state.[1] Similarly, the basic form of a narrative begins with an original state of affairs, describes actions or events as they unfold, and leads to a new state of affairs.[2] Narratives tell a story about what happened, or what should happen; they represent our understanding of reality, the way things are, or the way we would like things to be.[3]

Much of what we know is stored in narrative form—stories about why things are the way they are. Narratives plot events and draw relationships between them, implying both motives and causes. Narratives are ordered representations of our cognitive schema, the way we think. How do we attain this order? To make sense of our experience and arrive at explanations of "what happened," we create coherent stories about what happened and why. Existing narratives offer an explanation of what happened by looking back on events, but narratives also lay out guidelines for "what to do" when facing future events with similar circumstances. When we construct narratives out of our experience, we are crafting a response to a situation that can become a routine response.

Much of our cultural knowledge and values reside in and are shared via stories, such as "'The Boy Who Cried Wolf,'" which establishes a norm that we should not lie. Narratives are repositories of our knowledge, telling us how to act in certain situations. Our shared values are carried in popular narratives that outline the way things are, how they should be, and how we should act. Once we learn these narratives, they shape our understanding of events, and we use them to determine what we should do or how we should act in certain situations. Narratives condition us to see the world in particular ways, and how we see things determines how we act or respond. Applying an existing narrative determines our response. We do as the narrative directs us.

The cultural narrative "If you want something done right, do it yourself" entails values of rugged individualism and self-reliance. Narratives often contain causal logics that set our expectations: in this case, doing something all by yourself is the only way to accomplish anything. Seeking help is discouraged. Many of our most popular success stories are about individuals who have "pulled themselves up by their own bootstraps," improving their lives by getting out of bad circumstances without help. These stories socialize us to believe that success by our own efforts goes beyond assuming that you *can* do something by yourself to believing that you *should* do everything by yourself. The downside of this narrative is that it discourages us from asking for help when we need it. This is a significant downside, as you will see, because narratives control our behavior.

Narratives are the products of our collective sensemaking.[4] When we produce a narrative, we generate some view of the world.[5] If narratives become widely shared in a culture, they establish particular assumptions about how things should be, positing cause-and-effect logics that lead to some value-laden end. In addition to defining how things should be done, existing narratives serve as interpretive schema that we use to make sense of everyday events. We don't know what to think about a situation until we apply a narrative as an interpretive tool. All experience is filtered through narratives. We use narratives to define the situation—whether the event is good or bad in our culture—then use other narratives to guide our decisions about what to do.

We search our minds for narratives that tell us what to think and what to do in every situation we encounter. For example, I lived abroad on several occasions, and I encountered a unique cultural narrative to explain this event: When a bird poops on you, it is considered good luck! I do not know if I ever adopted the logic of this popular narrative (the logic of narratives often remains implicit or unspoken); I did not linger under building ledges hoping to be hit with some bird luck, but it did help me accept a few ill-timed pigeon droppings with a smile and a shrug. This particular narrative directs those who accept it to respond positively to something that otherwise may seem like a negative event. At the very least, people in those cultures have a grin and bear it attitude compared to my worldview, in which bird poop dropping on you could ruin your day. As we apply the same narratives to guide us through various experiences time and time again, they become so entrenched and widely accepted that they are taken for granted and never questioned. I don't know if I could be convinced of the logic statement that bird poop is good luck, but the assumption seems impervious to criticism: It's just good luck! In all cultures, some widespread narratives have a history that gives them this privileged status—they are unquestionable and beyond reproach. Some are so ingrained that even questioning them violates norms, but that is exactly what must happen if we are to pursue narrative change.

Challenging or changing entrenched narratives can be difficult, but it is also true that we create new narratives all the time. All narratives were created by us (where else could they come from?), and there is no reason to think we have suddenly stopped creating narratives and are stuck with the current story. For example, when novel events occur, we often craft a new narrative to help us make sense of the new situation and posit some appropriate action. Recognizing that we create and use narratives all the time is helpful because changing the way things are requires that we create a new narrative vision for how we want things to be. The logic blueprint for bringing the new vision into reality through action goes like this: If we do this, then that will happen. I use the term *narrative* to describe this process, and researchers confirm that having a compelling vision with a vivid description is crucial when leading change.[6]

Enacting new narratives to create transformational change is the central idea in this book. Narratives connect the normal to the extraordinary, creating a bridge from how things are to how they can be. Narratives explain and create deviations from the norm,[7] which is crucial when leading change. This narrative ability enables us to plot how our actions can lead to even the most extraordinary future state.

■ ■ ■

But there are challenges. To enact a new vision, we must break free from the control of the old way of doing things. One of the main differences of my approach from most theories of change is that I assert that the old way of doing things is much harder to overcome than these theories imply, if they discuss this at all. Before we get to enacting change, we must devote some attention to how the old institutionalized ways of doing things pressure us to conform.[8] We must resist these pressures. It is a substantial challenge.

The old way of doing things often has the status of an unquestioned norm, and we may not even be conscious of the narrative that directs us to do things the way they have always been done. The old way of doing things can become so entrenched that it guides us on autopilot. We follow the logic of the established narrative mindlessly, unaware of our conformity. Change implies nonconformity, and resisting the old way requires tremendous purposeful effort. The overlooked task of overcoming the current way of doing things is as difficult as, and a key aspect of, enacting change and establishing a new way of doing things.

Another main assumption I hold is that our actions are always guided by something—always. None of us has ever taken action based on nothing. It may be difficult to articulate, such as cultural norms, but our actions are guided even if this something is so deeply seeded, so *normalized*, that we do not realize we are going by it. Not being aware of the narrative ensures that we will remain stuck in our old ways. So the double whammy is that unquestioned narratives guide our actions, and we are not even aware of them.[9] In fact, we often remain stuck in our old way of doing things even when it no longer serves us and, yes, even when it becomes detrimental to us.

Whether conscious of it or not, members of organizations already have a way of doing things, even if their early practices amounted to little more than norms defined by default or happenstance. Established ways become more deeply institutionalized over time. Even narratives that grew out of a series of ad hoc responses are not easily dismissed. The old way of doing things has a powerful control over us, shaping how we think, act, and see things. Change is not as simple as creating a vision and putting it in place. Change does not take place in a vacuum.

Focusing on the things we are already doing provides a much-needed dynamic and reflexive view for transformation. My approach takes into account the pressure to conform to existing norms even as we try to change them. Change normally involves a confrontation between the old way and a new way, so learning how to fight against the old way is crucial when enacting change. As you will see, we are often unwitting participants in tightening the grip the old way has on us, even when we are trying to change. You may have heard it put this way: "You can't change the system; you're part of the system." This is a long-held paradox of change.[10]

How do we alter institutions, organizations, cultures, and communities even as they pressure us to conform to their norms? Although definitely a challenge, I believe that change from the inside is possible. In this book I describe how to conceptualize these complexities and outline how we might resist the control of institutions as we set about changing them. Any new narrative must fight against existing narratives to gain a foothold. By examining how narratives are created and become established or institutionalized, we can learn how to create and enact new ones.

To summarize, narratives guide how we think and act. As we navigate situations, we enact narratives. We may not be consciously aware of the narrative and the rules or norms it entails, but our actions stabilize narratives, and they become norms. Over time, what should be done in certain situations eventually becomes THE way things are done. For example, we have a narrative about the way things are done in elevators. We let people out before we get on; we step in, select our floor, and look toward the doors. This narrative entails several norms, and we adhere to them pretty strictly. We are probably on autopilot while enacting this narrative, and in this way narratives control us.

The big picture is that we can change the way we think and act, and we can change the way things are done, the way things are understood. Learning the social psychology behind narratives and the art of narrative change helps us meet this goal. My model of change helps you understand how you might loosen the control of existing narratives and enact new narratives that enable you to foster change. You will gain insights into how we got here, which is beneficial in providing a perspective on how norms and institutions form and then control us. That additional point of view is helpful in understanding what you are up against when enacting change.

One of the payoffs is that you will be able to apply these lessons to your organization, community, team, or your own life, immediately. You might also coach others and help them develop narratives for themselves, such as the personal leadership narratives I discuss later. If you are going to live by a narrative, you might as well be the one to create it. You will accomplish more of what you want to do.

I am giving you a powerful tool, but with powerful tools come strong cautions. My hope is that you will use this knowledge for good, but as you will come to see, it can be used toward less benevolent ends. You can attempt to control people by crafting new narratives that give you power over the way they act. My preferred goal is for you to become conscious of the narratives that govern your actions and to understand how others may have control over you.

I provide the tools you need to enact large-scale transformational change of any kind, from creating an entirely new culture for your organization or team to generating a concrete strategy for a social movement. Or you can start by changing yourself. The model of narrative change applies just as well to personal transformation as it does to large-scale change. Because the model is rooted in a description of how change happens naturally, you can use it not only to understand change or the way things are done but also to create new ways of doing things. Perhaps you just conform to "society," but even then, you might free yourself from narratives that constrain your possibilities. In fact, emancipation from controlling narratives may be more valuable than creating a new narrative, and this model will help you do both.

To illustrate the model of narrative change, I tell the unlikely but miraculous story of Texas's first permanent death penalty defense team. We brought about a large-scale transformational change in how the death penalty operates in Texas. I was lucky enough to be involved from the start with a small team of people in a new office charged with defending indigent defendants against the death penalty in Texas. What began as a ragtag group of misfits became an unstoppable team that managed to resist tremendous pressure to conform as we enacted a new way of doing things. Our success was nearly unimaginable.

We began in West Texas, where the State of Texas got the death penalty against the accused in capital trials more than 90 percent of the time. By the time my engagement with the team ended, our record was 70 wins and 1 death sentence. As the chief of the office put it to me two years after it all began, "Hans, if you had told me we would be this successful at the start of all this, no one would have believed you. I never imagined we would be this successful. No one did."

Throughout the book, I use Uber as a corporate illustration to examine organizational change using the narrative change model as a lens. Uber has gone through an upheaval, to say the least. The $70 billion ride-sharing company is grappling with several narratives that must change if they hope to survive. Uber faces a crisis that threatens the entire organization, and Uber's own corporate culture is largely to blame. Uber needs to change "who we are" and especially "the way things are done around here." I describe how they are using many of the same principles of the narrative change model to enact a much-needed trans-formational change. I chose Uber because many of you will be familiar with the challenges they face. Whether changes must be made to a powerful institution such as the death penalty, or a wayward company that faces dissolution, the narrative change model can help you understand and inspire change.

I have been all over the country and overseas sharing these narrative change methods in various contexts. I have been able to apply them with success in a variety of change settings: to change corporate cultures, to improve public services, to inspire innovation, to create brand narratives, and to develop new prod-ucts. Although I use my encounter with the death penalty and change at Uber as compelling examples, there are lessons for organizational, social, institutional, and even personal change. You can also use the model to inspire social movements that benefit society or to develop individual leaders inside your orga-nization. In this book, I explain the same narrative change model I used in all of these contexts and share the underlying philo-sophical perspectives.

Transformational change is never easy. Changing the death penalty took a toll on all of us. The work was tormenting, and everyone on the team witnessed and experienced many types of suffering. I visited death row, twice. Most death penalty defense attorneys burn out quickly. I felt that same stress, and my convictions were certainly tested. Anguish nearly crushed my psyche; my job was in jeopardy. And on that journey, I was often confronted with the ghosts of my own past. At the same time, my past gave me a perspective essential to understanding change.

Internal challenges are often part of leading transformational change. I share personal notes about how I addressed those challenges because I think these stories may be helpful in your own change endeavors. Transformational change is hard work, but even at the toughest points, I found the work to be restorative and fulfilling. Engaging in the change process changed me. It gave me an intense purpose, and the work was deeply rewarding.

Once I got involved in fighting the death penalty, I definitely felt driven to make a difference. Something was at stake for me as well. Looking back, I think those two things helped me overcome the challenges of change. When our convictions are tested, we stand at a turning point in pursuing change. Our convictions can crumble, and we may give up. But if we feel driven to make a difference and have something at stake—how things will be in the future—our convictions can become a source of strength as we become more determined to achieve change.

I often say that my involvement in the death penalty came out of the blue—it is true that it was quite unexpected—but there is another, just as plausible, explanation. Looking back, it is possible that I was on an inevitable collision course with the death penalty. That story explains how I came to study narrative theory in the first place and, coincidentally (or maybe it was fate), how I got to thinking narratives could be used to construct something better than a traditional strategy. Upon reflection, I also see how creating and enacting a new narrative saved me from a deadly affliction. In that collision course version of what happened, changing the system against long odds is what I had been wrought to do.

Every experience I had ever had, every failure, especially my failures, shaped me for the challenge I faced. In that version, my entire life prepared me for this journey, despite my own plan to go into hiding and isolate myself from the world. As I found out, sometimes your destiny finds you on the very road you take to avoid it.

1

No Place to Hide

I desperately wanted to disappear. I should have begun the workshop already, but I inched back toward the corner of the large meeting room in Lubbock, Texas. A voice in my head whispered that I do not belong here, that this job is too big for me, and that attempting to change a monstrous system like the death penalty is impossible. I felt out of place and suspected it was only dumb luck that brought me to this moment. On top of that, people's lives were on the line.

At that time, death penalty defense had gone poorly in Texas. Death penalties were handed down more than 90 percent of the time in capital trials in Texas, and 98 percent of the time in West Texas. We had launched the country's first permanent death penalty defense team, and the entire team was present along with additional experts who came to lend their minds and insights to this endeavor. There are many public defender offices in the United States, but ours was the only one in the country that exclusively handled death penalty cases.

We intended to rewrite the way the death penalty was defended. Twenty people were gathered in the room. They milled around, sipped coffee, and introduced themselves to each other. We were all meeting for a daylong narrative change workshop I had suggested as a way to introduce a new narrative for defending against the death penalty. Attorneys, mitigators, constitutional experts, and other death penalty defense experts had traveled in from all over Texas.

When this began, I was a newly minted assistant professor at Texas Tech University, in the business school, in the management department. When I say I don't know how I wound up in that room that day with all the major death penalty defense players in Texas, it's because I had a very different plan when I moved to Lubbock. I am not a lawyer, and I never had any interest in the death penalty. My plan was to disappear; I was trying to be a hermit professor. None of it was working out.

I am an ethnographer. When people hear the word *ethnographer*, they probably picture an anthropologist in weather-beaten khakis traveling to visit distant tribes, studying culture by living among tribe members and engaging in their rituals. At the extreme, the anthropologist may even become part of the tribe. People are not wrong to imagine that, but today's ethnography is a less romantic version—although it can be just as adventurous.

Organizational culture became a distinguishing factor in corporate performance in the 1980s.[1] In exploring why a strong corporate culture made such a difference in business, researchers borrowed ethnographic methods from their anthropology cousins to study corporate culture. Ethnographers treated corporations like not-so-distant tribes and embedded themselves in corporate settings. They observed and worked alongside employees to understand the culture of the firm: what it is like to work here, what it is like to be them, and how we do things around here. If you knew what kind of culture great companies had, you could attempt to instill that same culture in your own organization and become great as well. In the search for what made some companies excellent, organizational culture was recognized as the primary factor.

Better performance through better cultures was a main area of focus, but some ethnographers simply sought to describe what it is like inside an institution for the sake of knowing, without an agenda of improving performance. For example, ethnographers described what it's like to work in an auto factory, to serve in a police force, or to work in a slaughterhouse, to name just a few. They sought to reveal the inner workings and culture of these groups by becoming insiders in these contexts. For example, cops had their own language and informal yet powerful codes for their behavior.[2] Strong norms dictated how cops should cover for one another and have each other's back, both on and off duty.

I joined the death penalty defense team and became a member of that tribe so I could watch and learn and participate as much as possible as an insider. One of my main research aims was to describe the inner workings of the death penalty and how it worked in practice. This understanding would eventually become crucial in changing how it worked.

The team wanted to change the way the institution of the death penalty worked, and I agreed to help organize the team. I observed their work, went everywhere they went, and participated in any way I could. For instance, I strategized on cases, visited defendants, met with DAs and judges, and shadowed team members to learn their roles in defending against the death penalty. Ethnographers often attempt to remain invisible, studying social interaction from an arm's length to minimize influencing what they observe. In some ethnographic practices, researchers are encouraged to maintain objectivity and keep some social distance between themselves and research subjects. For lots of reasons, being a fly-on-the-wall observer would not do this time. Once we decided to rewrite the ways things are done in death penalty defense by constructing a collective narrative that the team would use in their daily work, it became impossible for me to maintain any distance. Ethnography of this type required me to get close to the culture to understand it. If we were going into battle together, I would have to become an insider.

■ ■ ■

Stares from around the room cajoled me to begin. Earlier that morning I had laid out a blank slate, with dozens of sheets of paper torn from giant flip charts. The pages were spread neatly across several folding tables, and I squeezed a fistful of markers to keep my hands from shaking. I began to speak. At the end of that day, our budding narrative was strewn all over the room, with more ink than white space on any piece of paper.

After hours of creative discussion and excited conversation, the room was finally quiet. I could hear the florescent lights hum above me. Exhausted, I crawled around on the floor, trying to put into order what amounted to a collective brain dump. Alone in the room, I made additional notes and sorted through all the pages we had filled. Every tattered page contained some kind of list, diagram, or scribbling about how we planned to fight the death penalty. The new narratives we would create from this material were the seeds for change.

■ ■ ■

My whirlwind encounter with the death penalty began with a cold call; I was asked to help design and build the country's first permanent death penalty defense team. I conducted a six-year ethnographic study of how the death penalty operates in practice, seeking to understand its inner workings and strategizing new ways to change the way things are done. All of my theoretical ideas about change were put to a real-world test. The stakes were life and death. I never became comfortable with the task, but I think that's a good thing.

We pursued a risky strategy using an innovative methodology I developed called *narrative construction*. We created a narrative to organize the team, to determine the work they would do, and to change the way the death penalty operates. A narrative perspective also helped us understand and make sense of what others did, such as district attorneys. Instead of a typical structure and strategy, our team used narratives to guide our actions and to decide what tactics to pursue in death penalty cases.

Skipping ahead six years, our ragtag team has stopped more than one hundred executions against nearly insurmountable odds. We also expanded the office, covering almost all of Texas. By the time my research engagement ended, we had lost only once. Today Texas sentences very few people to death (figure 1.1).

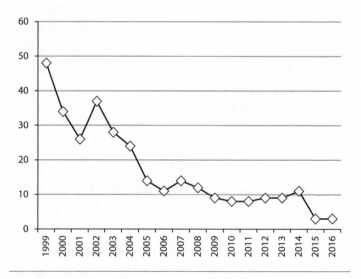

Figure 1.1 Death sentences in Texas, 1999–2016

Source: Chart by the author

In the years before I got the call, Texas sentenced more than forty people to death each year. In the past two years, only three people have been sentenced to death. Several factors have been at work, but our team has been a major component of this change. We have managed to change the way things work.

2
Talking Narratives

Seth Rose killed two people in Arkansas, stole their truck and some guns, and drove across Texas, heading for Mexico. He stopped for gas in the Panhandle in the middle of the night, and instead of getting back on the highway, he drove down a farm road into the darkness. Seth pulled up to a random farmhouse, went in with an AK-47, and killed the entire family of five; only one young boy, who played dead, survived. Seth shot the boy as he dove for his bed, blasting his body into the wall. He landed still and lifeless.

Seth got back in the truck and crossed the border into Mexico. Seth cannot really articulate why he went to Mexico, except that he knew that was where people went when they were on the run. Seth was going by a popular narrative. After Seth got to Mexico, he stayed in Juarez and simply drove around for a few hours. Inexplicably, Seth then headed back to Arkansas. As he crossed back into the United States, border agents in El Paso searched the truck and found the guns, and the officers discovered that the truck and guns were registered to the murdered couple in Arkansas.

Seth reached a plea bargain and was sentenced to two consecutive life without parole terms for the Arkansas murders.

He later told guards in the Arkansas prison that he was probably also wanted in Texas for killing a family there. They ignored him at first, and if not for Seth's persistence in confessing, the farmhouse murders would never have been solved.

Texas extradited Seth to face the death penalty. If Seth was sentenced to death there, Texas could kill him. If he got life without parole in Texas, Seth would be sent back to Arkansas to serve his two consecutive life sentences without parole there before serving his life sentence without parole in Texas. This really meant that Texas was hell-bent on killing Seth and was willing to waste a bunch of money trying to do so.

The trial was moved to Lubbock, and I consulted and assisted the defense team. On the first day of trial, the prosecution played the boy's 9-1-1 call. Through every kind of pain, the eleven-year-old struggled to describe the gruesome scene. His entire family, including the dog, had been killed.

After trial that day, I stayed behind in the empty courtroom with Seth, Seth's attorney, Andy, and the sheriff's deputies assigned to guard Seth. Seth sat in a chair we had moved to the center of the courtroom, just in front of the judge's desk. We needed to cut Seth's greasy mullet so he would look more presentable to the jury. For security reasons, the guards would not let us use scissors. Andy brought in a pair of electric clippers and a comb, and I commandeered an empty trash bag from under the judge's desk. Seth's mullet went halfway down his back. As Andy fumbled with the clippers, I held the plastic trash bag snug around Seth's neck with my thumbs and fingers stretched while I pulled the opposite side of the bag tight with my teeth. I tried to focus on catching the falling hair, but my mind kept picturing the jury's faces as they listened to the horrific 9-1-1 call. They exchanged glances between themselves and the floor, but never held eye contact.

"How is it looking?" Seth called back over his shoulder.

"Not good," I said.

■ ■ ■

James Neely murdered Ed Richardson in Midland, Texas. James and his girlfriend Candice only had one intention that night—to leave town. They had received an eviction notice at the apartment building where they were staying. James and Candice walked across the street to a bowling alley that night, and then down the street to a bar, roaming through parking lots, looking to steal a car. At the bar they approached a lady as she was leaving and asked her for a ride. Once in the car, they planned to force her out and take the vehicle. James had a silver butterfly knife in his pocket. Candice did the talking while James waited in front of the car, but the woman got skittish when they seemed unclear on exactly where they wanted to go. She slammed the door and left. James and Candice continued walking down the street. They saw Ed Richardson milling around his truck behind the plumbing store he owned.

"Hey mister," James called out, "can you give us a ride?" James had his arm around Candice.

"Where do you need to go?" Mr. Richardson was a World War II vet who would do just about anything for anyone. He had a soft spot in his heart for hitchhikers. As a young man in the service, he would hitchhike his way back and forth between Texas and his post in California.

"The Salvation Army," James said quickly.

The truck only made it 642 feet. James collared Mr. Richardson from behind with his left arm and tried to lift Mr. Richardson out of his seat. Richardson tried to wriggle out of James's grasp. With his right hand, James began to stab Richardson in the shoulder, neck, and face. Defensive wounds on his hands would show that Mr. Richardson blocked some of the stabs before Candice grabbed his arms and forced them into his lap. James continued to stab. Candice managed to extend her leg over and press the brake pedal, stopping the truck. More stabs landed. Mr. Richardson stopped fighting and slumped down into the driver's seat.

"Give me the keys and wallet!" James screamed.

Mr. Richardson reached into his back pocket and held up his wallet. Mr. Richardson's carotid artery and jugular vein had been cut. Blood poured out of him. It soaked his clothes and filled a plastic cup in the seat between him and Candice. Candice reached for the keys and yanked and yanked but could not get them out of the ignition. The truck was still in drive.

"Don't kill me son," Mr. Richardson murmured. He began to reach to put the truck in park and get the keys out of the ignition, but as he did his hand went limp and dropped into his lap. His blood pressure was so low he could no longer move his limbs. James stood and reached around Mr. Richardson. James dropped the knife to the floorboard as he twisted the ignition switch back and forth until he got the keys to release. James and Candice got out of the truck.

The interior dome light came on.

"There was so much blood," James would testify. Seeing it made him sick. Candice started down the street and screamed for James to run, but James stood aghast, looking into the open truck door.

While the jury deliberated whether or not to give James the death penalty, I sat with James at the defense table for a long while, trying to have idle conversation, telling him not to drive himself crazy with what more he could have said or done.

"You did just fine, James," I congratulated him on his testimony from the stand. James did not testify at his first trial.

This time, he detailed the night of the crime, took responsibility, and shared his remorse. He cried while he spoke, as men cry, his face suddenly wet, his voice shaky and cracking.

"I just told the truth," James kept saying.

I tried to change the subject. During court recess earlier that day, I had taken James's mother and sister to lunch. They asked me to tell him that they were proud of him and wanted me to make sure that he knew that. I told him. When he mentioned the jury, I told him again.

That morning James's mother and sister, who had travel from out of state to the trial, got the chance to talk with him. Our team had arranged a brief visit in an otherwise empty courtroom. After the jury had been dismissed for lunch, the guard let James's mother and sister stay behind and visit James. James sat at the defense table, where he usually stayed during any courtroom breaks. His mother and sister sat on the gallery side, but they leaned on the banister separating the gallery and the defense table. James had swiveled around in his chair. At one point, they held hands. The guard leaning against the wall had straightened up and glared at this touching, but said nothing.

The meeting was against protocol, but we had convinced the guard to give us five minutes. Five minutes turned into ten. Toby, the first chair attorney on James's case, had asked me to stay close by, monitor the conversation, and just be present "in case something goes wrong." I had no idea what I was supposed to do, not just in case but especially if something went wrong.

"What's gonna go wrong?" I asked. My eyes slowly landed on each of the three guns I could see in the courtroom, one on the hip of each deputy.

"Just watch closely and take notes of everything that happens," Toby said.

"Oh," I sighed in relief. "That's all I ever do."

Soon enough, the nearest guard signaled to me that time was up. I caught James's eye and nodded to him. James stood up and began to back away from the banister. His mother stood too, but then she suddenly lurched forward. She hugged James and pulled him into her chest. The guard took a quick step toward us, then stopped. The guard later confided that he had a brother in prison and could empathize with James's mother. James's mother held him tight. When she let go, she was crying. Her body shook as I led her out of the courtroom.

When I got his mother and sister into my car, James's mother stared straight ahead for a long while. "That's the first time I have touched my son in twenty years," she said.

▪ ▪ ▪

"The jury has been out a long time," James said to me as we continued to wait in the courtroom that evening. "You've seen a lot of these, is that good or bad?"

I had no idea. There was just no telling. I told James I would never hazard a guess, and that even contemplating what might be going on in that room would only drive us crazy. I told him I had heard lots of anecdotal evidence, but the stories all contradicted each other. Some people say it is good if the jury is out a long time, some say it is a bad sign. I told him I would not read anything into it. It was not the time to correct James, but despite his crediting me with lots of experience, I had never waited for a jury to make a life or death decision before this. James had done it twice. He just wanted to hear something, anything, that could be interpreted as a good sign. He wanted hope.

Sometimes hope is a cruel thing to give a man.

▪ ▪ ▪

My fight against the death penalty began with a cold call to the antiquated phone in my university office (the phone was original equipment from when the building opened in 1966). The call startled me because I had been in the Management Department at Texas Tech just over a year and that phone had never rung. I did not even know the number. The plastic piece of junk rattled and blared in its faded cradle several times before I even realized the phone was ringing. I also did not immediately speak when I picked up the handset, intending to examine it rather than answer it.

"Hello?" a voice finally scratch-echoed from the tin earpiece as I stared at it.

I slowly pressed it to my ear. "Can you hear me?"

"Hello?" said the caller. "Whom am I speaking to?"

"Hans Hansen," I said. "Who were you looking for?"

Michael Block and I made plans to meet later that week at a place called The Coffee Haus on University Avenue, right across from the Texas Tech campus. Michael had cold called the Management Department looking for "anyone who knew something about team building." Research on teams is a distinct and vibrant area of research, but I was not familiar with any of it. Michael said someone suggested he try me.

"It's the first team of its kind," Michael said on that phone call. He briefly described a team made up of lawyers who were used to doing their own thing. "They've always been lone wolves, but now we have to get them to work together." I agreed to meet, but I told him up front that I would be directing him to someone else once I got a few more details.

When I walked into the coffee shop, Michael was already there. He brought along Walter Kape, who had been picked to head the new office, which would officially open the following month. We huddled around a bistro table in the tiny storefront.

At Michael's request, I had sent him a paper explaining a little about what I do. It was from a dense academic journal, but it described both ethnography and narrative theory, my methodology and my main theoretical approach. He had shared it with Walter.

"I needed a thesaurus to read it," said Michael.

"I read the parts that were in English," joked Walter.

I could hardly blame them. Academic journal articles can be pretty dry—crumbling, actually. Although I was in a business school, I pointed out that I used ethnography because qualitative methods are suited to the kinds of topics I study, such as organizational culture. I held back from sharing that qualitative research was not very popular in business schools where quant jocks often ruled the roost.

A qualitative approach to research posits that the best way to gain knowledge is through firsthand experience of the phenomena. If you want to know what skydiving is like, for example, you go skydiving, whereas researchers using other approaches may send surveys to a hundred skydivers in an attempt to measure their experience. Both approaches have strengths and weaknesses.

Qualitative researchers studying culture, for example, make firsthand observations of cultural practices, customs, and rituals, and they even participate in the culture to the extent that they can. In the golden days of anthropology, an ethnographer might live in a foreign culture and participate in their customs and rituals. Ethnographers make an effort to have a firsthand encounter with whatever they are studying. They take field notes about the social interactions they observe and interview members of groups about rules and rites of passage in their society. They try to elicit unspoken cultural rules and norms so they can describe "how things work" in a particular culture.

Organizational researchers do the same thing with companies. Just like their cultural anthropologist forebearers, organizational ethnographers observe or work in organizations so they can describe what it's like in that setting. Ethnographers study norms by observing corporate rituals such as sales meetings, where outstanding customer service behaviors and others are rewarded with titles like Employee of the Month. Or perhaps they get a job at a car factory to gain insight into the informal rules of working on an assembly line.

Corporate narratives tell us a lot about an organization's culture. We have all heard stories about behaviors that are celebrated or sanctioned in the places we have worked. For example, people who work all night may be lauded, whereas people who question the authority of the boss are fired on the spot. Perhaps you have heard about the proverbial hardworking CEO who is still the first one in the office every day and the last one to leave each night. We hear stories about employees who go to extraordinary lengths to satisfy customers. Perhaps a new manager is brave enough to cancel a high-profile product launch at the eleventh hour because the product did not meet the company's standards. Instead of being fired, the new manager is immortalized in company folklore for her insistence on quality. Stories like these are told over and over in companies so employees know what is important in that culture and to encourage, we might even say control, behavior. Stories help socialize newcomers and model the norms that make up the culture in a way more memorable than any corporate policy manual.

▪ ▪ ▪

"So where will this new team be? What will they be doing?" I asked Michael and Walter.

"It will be right here in Lubbock," Michael said. The new team would cover most of West Texas. The new office would serve as a public defender's office, but only for death penalty cases. Michael and Walter gave me a primer on how the death penalty usually works. They were both experienced and had tried many death penalty cases, some together. Overall, things had not gone well with death penalty defense in Texas. "The State wins over 90 percent of the time," Walter said. I was flabbergasted at the time, but now that I know how it works, I am shocked that the percentage was not even higher.

To be certain you will get the death penalty in Texas, you have to kill at least two people, a child under six years old, or a cop. "If you kill a cop, they'll break the bank to kill you," Michael said. You can also get the death penalty for murdering someone in the course of another crime, such as a rape-murder or murder in the course of a burglary.

Of course, not every murder results in the death penalty. The DA is supposed to consider a list of aggravating factors, but in reality the odds of getting the death penalty depend less on any aspect of the crime itself than on the race of the victim and the defendant. The heinousness of the murder is supposed to be a factor, but nothing appears to be more heinous than minorities killing white people. The social status of the victim is probably the largest determinant in whether a murderer is charged with the death penalty, and in the United States, with our history, social status is still too closely tied to race. For people on death row in Texas, all else being equal, their victim was white more than 70 percent of the time and black just 11 percent of the time. Texas seeks "more justice" when whites are killed because the justice system deems white lives to be worth more than black lives.

In late 2011, Texas executed Lawrence Brewer for the infamous dragging death of James Byrd Jr.[1] Brewer and his codefendants were white supremacists. They chained James Byrd behind a pickup truck and dragged him along the road until his body tore apart. Lawrence never showed remorse, and if he had the chance, he said he would do it again. Texas executed him.

It was the first time that Texas had ever killed a white person for killing a black person.

■ ■ ■

"So the new team will replace the current court-appointed defense system?" I asked.

"Yes," Walter said, "but only for death penalty cases. We will be the permanent death penalty defenders."

"If there's a death penalty case, it will be ours," said Michael. "For other types of cases, the court will continue to appoint attorneys just like they do now."

When someone is charged with a crime, if the person cannot afford an attorney, the court appoints one. If it is a death penalty case, that attorney has to be death penalty qualified. Similar to medical specialists, capital certified attorneys have to have additional experience, training, and continuing education to qualify them to do the highly specialized work of death penalty cases. As part of his responsibilities for the Texas Criminal Defense Lawyers Association, Michael organized continuing education training for lawyers seeking to become death penalty qualified.

The pool of certified capital attorneys in Texas had been dwindling for several years. "In some jurisdictions, you just needed a bar card and a pulse to take a death penalty case," Michael said. Incompetent attorneys were being appointed to death penalty cases by judges who did not care. Texas has made national headlines for using defense attorneys who have slept through capital trials, to name just one popular example.[2]

In the past decade, appellate courts have ordered retrials for capital cases when defendants have had ineffective counsel. Sometimes the lawyers did not present mitigating evidence or call experts that may have changed the outcome of the trial. Sometimes lawyers failed to file routine motions to exclude prosecution evidence. And, yes, sometimes they fell asleep during a trial when someone's life was on the line.

Texas seemed immune to the embarrassment but not to the increasing expense of footing the bill for all those retrials. Giving someone a retrial means an entire do-over, a clean slate. A retrial costs just as much as the original trial, and perhaps more if it is done right the second time. Courts hate spending money to have someone sentenced to die twice just because of some amateur snafu. The Texas legislature was getting agitated about the expenses.

One fix was to increase the training requirement for attorneys to be death penalty certified. There were also new resources, such as the Capital Case Bench Book, to assist judges presiding over capital cases. That book identified common issues and gave judges direction as to what is legally required in capital cases. The American Bar Association developed guidelines for capital cases, which most courts adopted, such as requiring a defense team made up of two attorneys, a fact investigator, and a mitigator. On its face, these changes would seem to help, but Texas did not increase the amount they paid attorneys to take capital cases. Texas often paid attorneys a flat fee of $25,000 to take a death penalty case.

There is no bigger case than a death penalty case. They are long, drawn-out juggernauts that require all your time, effort, and attention. If you have a capital case, it should be a priority. Cases often take years to resolve, even if you reach a plea. Death penalty cases are not for the faint of heart.

Attorneys on court appointment lists usually have their own private practice to run in addition to making themselves available on the public defender roster. The appointment process varies across jurisdictions. Sometimes judges appoint attorneys, and cronyism and campaign contributions can play a role in who is assigned to death penalty cases. Sometimes there is a list and a court administrator simply appoints the next lawyer in line. Sometimes they literally spin a wheel to see whose name comes up. If the attorney has a private practice that is going gangbusters and has plenty of money coming in, the attorney may turn down the case. Who wants to put everything on hold for three years to take a death penalty case, especially when you are only paid $25,000 to do the whole thing?

In fact, two types of attorneys take that kind of work: the very best and the very worst. The very best are ideological, true believers who do whatever it takes to focus on saving someone's life. The worst are doing so poorly in their private practice that the $25,000 flat fee looks attractive. They often take a death penalty case alongside trying to manage their private practice, doing divorces, DWIs, and whatever work they can bill. Because they get a flat fee, there is no incentive to put time into the case. In fact, there is an incentive to put in as little time as possible, thereby increasing the amount of money earned per hour (billable hours is how revenue is measured in the legal world). So defendants get lawyers who take on death penalty cases but don't devote any time to them, and don't care, because the state wins all the time anyway.

"Some of them might as well be pall bearers," Michael said.

If an attorney does not want to take a death penalty case, the judge or administrator spins the wheel again or calls the next attorney on the capital-qualified list. The judge may have to call several attorneys before one agrees to take the case. In some

Texas counties, only two or three people are on the list. When Texas increased the certification requirements, but not the compensation, the list of certified attorneys dropped dramatically. Why put in more time and effort to maintain your death penalty certification if the pay does not change? The work is thankless and tormenting. If you care, you feel responsible for someone's life. Most people do not last long under that kind of pressure.

As late as the mid-2000s, more than seven hundred attorneys were qualified to take death penalty cases in Texas. On the day Michael called me, there were less than seventy.

The lack of death penalty certified attorneys was especially bad in rural West Texas. Judges would demand that Michael, who happened to live in Lubbock, find someone to take a capital case because of his role with capital assistance at the Texas Criminal Defense Lawyers Association. "Who's on your list?" Michael would ask the judge.

"He was too busy," said the judge. "Get me someone else." Or maybe the attorney had angered the judge somehow: hadn't contributed to the judge's reelection campaign or was combative on some other case. Or maybe the attorney really was too busy, doing too well in private practice to want to put everything on hold for years to take on a soul-retching death penalty case.

Meanwhile, there was pressure from outside Texas to get things in order. Next door, in Louisiana, they were having similar problems appointing attorneys to defend capital cases. Higher courts told Louisiana that they were serious about the constitutional rights to a defense. If Louisiana was not able to provide a defense against the death penalty, these courts pointed out that Louisiana could no longer charge people with it.

Bloodthirsty Texas took notice. With judges breathing down his neck to get more attorneys certified to do death penalty cases, Michael made an innovative suggestion. "What if we had a permanent capital defense team?" Michael asked. Then no one would have to worry about appointing attorneys to capital cases anymore.

No more judicial appointments. No more lists. No more wheels. If the district attorney charged someone with the death penalty, the case would automatically go to the public defender team for capital cases. The team would handle only death penalty cases, but all of the death penalty cases, across a large geographic area. It would be like an anti-DA's office. The district attorney's office is a permanent office in charge of prosecuting crimes. We could have a permanent office in charge of defending crimes, but only death penalty cases.

Administrative judges in Texas talked, the Task Force for Indigent Defense got involved, and they decided to start the capital defense office as an experiment, based in West Texas. A big part of the task force's concern was providing indigents' defense for death penalty cases because those cases are so high-profile and come under so much scrutiny from higher courts— not to mention the media.

We named the new office the West Texas Regional Public Defender for Capital Cases. It was supposed to be an experiment lasting a few years, and it was meant to serve only two of the nine Texas judicial administrative regions, in which capital case appointments had been particularly challenging. The team took all the capital cases from the seventh and ninth judicial regions, which covered the entire Panhandle of Texas, all the way down to Midland and Odessa, and west over to Pecos and east past Abilene, an area that included more than eighty counties and almost a third of Texas.

In line with the American Bar Association guidelines, the new team would be made up of attorneys, mitigators, and a fact investigator. There would be office staff. For death penalty cases, the courts mandate two attorneys, a first and second chair, for each death penalty defendant. Mitigation specialists and fact investigators assist with various investigations to support the defense. Some judges in Texas were hesitant to adhere to the guidelines because it was not a good look politically to spend taxpayer money defending killers. Typical Texans were not eager to hear about their tax dollars being used to defend murderers.

Counties signed on in droves. Not having to fork over taxpayer money to pay for the defense anymore was mouthwatering. Instead of paying the entire cost of providing a defense, counties would now pay a nominal fee and have all the death penalty defense team expenses covered in the event of a capital case.

Counties referred to our office as providing "murder insurance." Each county paid a little bit every year to avoid a big expense in the event of the catastrophic costs of a death penalty case. For rural counties, a death penalty case could wipe out the entire budget. Capital case expenses lasting several years can easily reach a million dollars once you add up the prosecution, investigation, defense, defense investigation, and mitigation costs, not to mention the costs to pay for expert testimony on both sides, and other court costs such as seating a jury. No matter where a killing occurs, the defendant is entitled to an effective defense, and the local government must cover all of these costs, even if the county is dirt poor. With the new team in place, the appointment problems would be gone and the cost would be controlled. It was very attractive financially. No one gave much thought to whether we would win or not. Given the past record, why should that enter anyone's mind?

So far, Walter had been the only person hired. "So how do we go about building the team?" Michael asked me.

"Well, I'll try to find somebody who can help you," I said. "Most people—and they are smart people—might suggest coming up with a strategy and talking about things like hierarchy, mission statements, job descriptions, and team composition." Michal and Walter nodded. Those were the first terms out of my mouth they recognized.

"But I wouldn't do any of that stuff," I said.

Michael and Walter glanced at each other. "Well . . . what would you do?"

"I would create a team narrative. I would have the whole team collectively write a whole new narrative about the way we should defend death penalty cases. All the team members will have a role in the story, and our story will detail who is doing what when, and why, and what other team members are doing at every stage of a case. I would even include people outside of the team in a new narrative, like the DA and judges, to include the actions that others typically take during a death penalty case because they play a role in the narrative too. We must take into account the likely actions of others. All of those other voices will be included alongside the team's voice. That's one major departure from a typical strategy, which focuses on what an organization wants to do and how. If we're going to be interacting with the opposition during real cases, that needs to be represented in a team narrative."

"So we would start fresh?" Walter asked.

"In some ways," I said, "but we will still rely on all your experience and knowledge, and fashion a new narrative out of that existing material, putting it together in new ways. We will come up with some new ideas as well. We have a chance to literally rewrite the way the death penalty is defended."

"So what exactly is a narrative?" Michael asked. "Is it like a playbook?"

"You could say that," I said, "but a very descriptive one. It's more like a story, or a vision with a plan for bringing it to fruition. We would use the narrative to guide our actions and decisions. I like the phrase 'go by.' A team narrative is something we would *go by* in doing our work."

I told Michael and Walter that I often used the metaphor of a first date to explain narratives to my students. In class this past semester, I asked the class if anyone recalled going on their first date. I got a few reluctant hands. "Well, if you'd never done it before, how did you know what to do on your first date?" I ask. "How did you know how to behave?"

"I don't know," they say, "I guess from what I saw on TV and in movies."

"Yes," I say, "or maybe you had friends who had gone on dates who told you stories about what they did. What you do on a date involves cultural norms, right?"

There are nods.

"So before your date, is it safe to say you already have a narrative to 'go by' to guide your actions and help you accomplish the date?" More nods. I pick someone. "So what did you do on your first date?"

"Dinner and a movie," he said.

"The always reliable dinner and a movie. So that was a plan, right? And one you didn't think up on your own?"

They nod.

"You heard that narrative somewhere, right, your friends had done it? We might say that when we 'go by' a narrative, we are 'enacting' it into being, such that the narrative in our heads, our cognitive framework, comes to fruition and becomes reality as we act it out."

There are nods.

"By enacting the narrative, it becomes true, right? You actually perform the narrative into existence. It is an accomplishment. Like implementing a plan, we go by the narrative we have in our minds, and in doing so, it becomes reality and we end up going to dinner and a movie on a date."

More nods. I have them part way to understanding narrative theory.

"So narratives are handy, right? They allow us to navigate social situations such as first dates by enacting some narrative we hold. But what else do narratives do beside help us accomplish interactions like dates, or even job interviews?"

Silence.

"Do you see how the narratives we go by might also control us?"

They know that's a rhetorical question.

"What I mean is, narratives guide our behaviors, but they also control us, confining us to do things we think are appropriate in a particular situation. We follow social norms about dating. So what happens? Narratives guide us and allow us to accomplish a date, but . . . ?" I raise my eyebrows.

"We never do anything but go to dinner and a movie?" someone ventures.

"Exactly!" I say. "If our narrative defines a date as dinner and a movie, that is what we always do, over and over. Narratives can confine us, even imprison us!" I shout, "to a narrow set of behaviors. And if we keep enacting the same old narratives, we end up trapped in a cycle where we keep doing things the same old way. In fact, the narratives we go by can become so powerful that we can't imagine doing things any other way. Some narratives are so culturally ingrained and taken for granted that it never even occurs to us that we can do something other than go to dinner and a movie. We are on autopilot."

I try to walk and move my arms like a vacant-eyed robot. Everyone in the classroom is staring at me. That's good.

"It gets juicier," I say. "So narratives guide us, but also control us. Now, on top of that, we may never even realize this predicament because we are often not conscious of the narratives we are going by. You are always, whatever you're doing, going by something. And that something is guiding you, but it is also controlling you. And most of the time, we are not conscious we are being controlled. When we are mindlessly enacting our narrative of a date, we are not thinking about how it is just a cultural convention, learned through stories, that we are going by. We are thinking—that's just the way we do things. We don't critically question the origin or legitimacy of the narrative because we can't—because we don't even realize we're going by it."

I can see from my students' faces that wheels are starting to turn in their heads.

"So we can't question the narratives if we aren't conscious we are going by them. And we're being controlled via our own enactment of the narratives that society has indoctrinated us with. We strictly follow the narrative and the social norms they entail, without question, doing and thinking whatever they tell us to do. You are all basically programmed robots." I pause. "The bottom line is this: you're all doomed. Now have a good night. Go do whatever society or your TV tells you to do."

"So that's it?" someone frets. "We're leaving it right there? At we're doomed?"

"We only have two more minutes left," I say. "We have to leave it at doomed. It's a cliffhanger."

There are disapproving looks.

"Okay then, one last question!" I say. "But you all have to start thinking. Where do all these narratives come from? How do we get them?"

Puzzled looks.

"Well, they weren't always there, right? We had to learn them from somewhere."

"They come from us?" someone awakens.

"Yes, yes!" I say, "Us! Collectively. Society. We create them! We build them out of past experience and as we make sense of events, or come up with explanations of why things happen, or what should happen, by . . . ?"

"Creating narratives," someone finishes.

"Yes! Narratives are socially constructed, meaning that we, society, create them. Some narratives become so deeply ingrained and widely shared in our culture that they seem to be permanent and objective fixtures, like immutable laws of the universe about how things work instead of something we made up. But, if we are the ones who created the narratives, that means . . . ?"

"We can change them?"

"Bravo!" I put both arms up. "We can be free!"

There are smiles.

"Plus," I add, "narratives are changing all the time anyway, even if it is slow. Our social norms about dating are not the same as they were fifty years ago. Yes, there are still a lot of dinners and movies, but some tiny things have changed, like who pays, and who can ask whom out on a date. The good news is, if we created the narratives we go by, that means you can create a new narrative to go by, and attempt to enact it. You don't have to walk around like a robot doing whatever society has programmed you to do. Just remember, everyone else will be enacting various narratives as well, and you will be pressured to stick to the script. It can be a lot of pressure, and not always for good reasons."

"Just because that's the way it's always been done," says a student.

"Yes," I say, "norms. The social pressure to keep reenacting them seems insurmountable. So it won't be easy to enact a new narrative, but it is a possibility." I raise a finger for a final instruction. "You don't have to be controlled. You can be conscious and reflexive instead."

■ ■ ■

Michael, Walter, and I are the last three customers in the coffee shop. What I underlined for them was the idea that, if we go by narratives all the time, we should create the very narratives that we use to guide our behaviors and actions. We can take processes that we do naturally and unconsciously in everyday life and engage in them very deliberately and consciously on an organizational scale. Why shouldn't the team create and agree to go by our own narrative in deciding "how things are done" on death penalty cases?

"We'll play by our rules, not theirs," I said.

"There won't be any hugs or trust falls, will there?" Walter asked.

"Not unless you need a hug," I said. "I know it sounds weird, but if you think about it, enacting a narrative is not so different from pursuing a strategy. However, I believe thinking in narrative terms has a bunch of advantages over traditional vision statements or strategies. The very process of constructing the new narrative will give everyone on the team a shared understanding of what we're trying to accomplish, along with more details about how to go about it. Plus, they will have a better understanding of their role in enacting the narrative."

"So it will just be like a goal?" Michael asked.

"Much more powerful," I said. "Narratives entail goals as well as how to go about achieving them. I think stories provide a lot more direction than strategies but also retain a lot of flexibility. It will empower team members to act more proactively, yet their actions will be highly coordinated with other team members."

"Proactive would be nice," Michael said. "That's not something we see on many defense teams." Walter described how the DA drives things and the defense team is always reacting. "It would be nice to be on the offensive for once."

I closed by telling them I thought creating a narrative could instill a positive culture as well. I expected Walter and Michael to ask me when I could get them the name of somebody else to help them, so I could go right back to being a hermit in my office, writing papers that nobody would ever read, in journals that nobody ever heard of, all of which I had already resigned myself to do. To tell you the truth, I actually looked forward to it.

"We'll do it," said Michael.

My eyebrows shot up and my eyes widened. I am pretty sure my mouth opened a bit.

"Well, whatever we're doing now isn't working," Michael said.

Then, it got less flattering. "At this point, we're willing to try anything," said Walter.

"We'll do anything you tell us to, Hans. We'll create one of these narratives and use it to guide all our work. Just tell us what to do."

My tongue dropped toward my stomach as realization shot up my spine. I felt like a tremendous bluff had been called. Before that moment, the discussion had been comfortably theoretical.

"What's in it for you?" asked Walter.

Despite being flabbergasted, I managed to answer what would be in it for any academic. "Well, for me, I am in the publish-or-perish business, so whatever I do has to have a research component. I would like to conduct an ethnography of the death penalty. That means I need to learn about everything you do, go everywhere you go, and gain an insider's perspective on the death penalty."

"That will expose you to a lot of privileged information," Walter said.

"In that case," said Michael, "you had better just join the team."
Walter nodded.

"Do you have any legal experience at all?" Michael asked.

"None."

"I want to teach you your first legal term," Michael smiled, "pro bono."

"I've heard of it," I said. "Research will be my agenda, not money. I'll write papers about the death penalty as a social institution. I could do a paper about the narrative process we go through."

They smirked at each other.

"You won't have to read them! But just so you know, some professor-types would actually find it quite interesting. If we construct a team narrative and attempt to enact it, it will be the first time anyone has ever deliberately applied narrative theory as an organizing principle and strategic device. I think we would be the first organization anywhere to even try it."

Michael leaned forward, "You mean you've never done this?"

3

How the Change Model Emerged

My ideas about narrative change came from a setting much less distressing than the death penalty process. I was introduced to the power of narrative during a research engagement at the world-famous comedy theater, *The Second City*, in Chicago. When I was there, Tina Fey was the head writer, creating sketch comedy similar to what most people would recognize as the five- to ten-minute skits seen on *Saturday Night Live*.

In addition to comedy shows, Second City Communications provided programs for organizations that supported their company's agenda through themes and messaging in the comedy skits. After one such show, a telecom company executive related a surprising result.

"Do you remember the skit when they had me discussing the merger with a manager from the other company?" the executive asked.

"I do," I said.

"Well, in that scene, which was completely made up, they had me and the other manager jogging through a park as we discussed some merger issues."

"Yes," I recalled, "and as you jogged along and talked, you encountered and overcame all kinds of obstacles."

"The actors were running through a jungle, then a desert, over mountains, and stuff like that. It was funny."

"So that skit resonated with the employees?" I asked.

"It did!" he exclaimed. "But in an odd way. They all think I am a runner."

"And are you?"

"No, I've never run a day in my life. I hate running," he said.

"So how did you find out that they thought that?"

"They give me gifts! All kinds of running gear. I get shoes, running shorts, special watches, and gift cards to running stores. People forward me information about marathons! It's crazy."

In addition to serving as a proving ground for comedy legends John Belushi, Bill Murray, John Candy, Chris Farley, and, more recently, Steve Colbert and Tina Fey, Second City was also a proving ground for my ideas about narrative theory. I spent about eight months there doing an ethnography focused on how organizations construct stories to create shared understandings. I focused on how these corporate skits were created, and I conducted participant observation in the writer's room, where writers met with clients to discuss their meeting agenda, such as a merger announcement, and what the clients hoped the show might achieve for their company or organization.

My research was conducted in a division called Second City Communications, now Second City Works. They used their improvisation methods to deliver team building, communication, and leadership workshops to organizations. They also performed sketch comedy shows at corporate events, using skits to convey corporate strategy, culture, and messaging to employees. I studied how the writers and corporate clients crafted scripts to be performed in front of employees. The skits either framed current events or offered designs for the future, such as what the corporation should do, how employees should act, and what kind of culture they should have. The skits were perfect examples of what organizational researchers called organizational narratives.

At that time, organizational scholars doing narrative research collected and examined existing narratives, such as mission statements, letters to shareholders, and corporate histories. In analyzing these existing narratives, most researchers used methods such as discourse analysis to make inferences about the corporation's culture and identity. What I observed was groundbreaking research within narrative theory. Instead of interpreting existing narratives, I watched how narratives were created. Observing the narrative construction process as it happened was eye-opening. It allowed me to explore corporate decisions about what to include or exclude in each narrative, and how the company hoped a new narrative might change the corporate culture, achieve a shared understanding, or get everyone on the same page in pursuing a strategy. My research was the first to examine "the making of" stories and narratives with a focus on how narratives might create—not just reflect—corporate culture.

Besides being fun, *The Second City* was an extremely interesting and poignant research setting for narrative theory. My research got attention from some foundational members in the field of organizational narratives, including David Boje, a well-known academic authority on organizational narratives and storytelling.[1] He agreed to be on my dissertation committee, and along with Dan Spencer at the University of Kansas, they directed my attention to a critical postmodern approach to organizing, which entails a reflexive approach to critically analyzing how discourse creates reality.

On the day of my dissertation defense, my chairperson at The University of Kansas said the committee would be honored if David Boje would be the first to comment on my presentation. Professor Boje was very brief. He declared my work a unique success and explained why. After that, no one on my committee had much to say. My dissertation defense was over. Everyone's coffee was still hot.

■ ■ ■

I never intended to study narratives in the first place. The year prior to my work at *The Second City* in Chicago I was living in France, teaching management at the Ecole Supérieure de Commerce in Clermont-Ferrand. My main purpose for going to France was to get permission to conduct an ethnography at Michelin Tire headquarters, which was considering a new tire factory in recently privatized Russia. I had previously lived and taught in Russia, and I had established a contact at Michelin. I hoped to do an international management dissertation on French-Russian cross-cultural issues surrounding the opening of the new manufacturing plant. I spent six months having meetings about having meetings but made little progress at Michelin or at any tire plant in Russia. Having failed to secure a research setting, I slunk back to Kansas with my tail between my legs, pushing my PhD program into its fifth year.

On a lark, a friend from Chicago suggested I look into Second City's corporate division. I had never heard of it, but I was desperate for a research site and drove to Chicago to meet with the cofounder of Second City Communications, Joe Keefe. I pitched Joe my idea about studying corporate culture through the narratives (skits) they crafted.

"I kind of become part of your 'tribe,'" I explained in his office overlooking the intersection of North and Wells in Chicago. "As an ethnographer, I come here and 'live' among you and see what you do and what that's like. Over time, some patterns or themes should emerge that allow me to theorize about what is happening as these narratives are constructed and clients use them to various ends. Participant observation means that I watch everything that happens, take copious notes, ask lots of questions, and participate as fully as possible in the work context to understand all the processes."

"I have no idea what you just said, but you sounded great!" Joe said. "Let's find you someplace to sit."

One of the first narrative construction processes I observed was for a large Fortune 500 telecom company. The telecom company hired Second City Communications after they bought a smaller internet company that had been a fierce competitor. During the day, employees from both companies heard about plans for integrating the two former competitors. The two companies had very different cultures, but management thought they could retain the best parts of each organizational culture.

Second City works closely with clients to coauthor scripts that include content the client wants to communicate to its audience. Members of management meet at Second City headquarters to lay out their vision and agenda for the event, and Second City writes skits that support that agenda. Several treatments are presented, and the client selects three of the treatments to go to full script for the show. The final performance is a high-quality theatrical production, complete with a large stage, lighting effects, and music.

At the telecom merger meeting, one of the comedy skits performed showed members from the previously separate companies adrift in a life raft. Humorous caricatures illuminated and exaggerated the differences between the characters with satire that represented the cultural differences between the companies. The skit opened with an old man and a "young whippersnapper" stranded at sea together in the life raft. They each claimed to know what was best and insisted on paddling in different directions. Their chaotic struggling and splashing was outdone only by their bickering. The old man and the young whippersnapper learned a thing or two from each other, and each came to appreciate what the other had to contribute. In the end, the characters decided to overcome their own interests and work together in harmony. This, of course, resulted in their triumph and survival.

This short organizational narrative mirrored management's contention that their survival depended on the two companies overcoming their cultural differences and developing an ability to work together following restructuring after the merger. The meetings and the show presented a new narrative for the company, but a lot remained to be seen, such as whether or not the new narrative would be enacted by employees.

A few weeks after the show, I met with that executive at the telecom company and asked how the merger was going. I also asked whether he thought the show had helped create a shared understanding among employees about the merger and integrating their cultures.

"I think so," he said. Some lines from the skit about the differences in culture had become inside company jokes, along with an appreciation of those differences. Then he related the story about his employees believing he was a runner based on the portrayal in one of the skits, and that had really shocked him.

"Well, it seems like something really stuck," I said. Regardless of the truth, the narrative had created a reality for employees—a vision real enough that they acted on it.

"And moreover," he continued, "they think my counterpart at the other company and I are lifelong running buddies. I never met him until the merger process began, but everyone assumes we ran track together or something as kids. It's amazing."

"That's pretty powerful," I noted. "You can only hope that all the messages about coming together as a single company were taken just as seriously."

"If so," he nodded, "this merger will be a breeze."

Something powerful was happening as a result of the organizational narratives presented to the employees. Although the manager being a running enthusiast was not "true," it was true for the employees. The narrative had created a bit of reality for them. That day I realized that organizational narratives were being underutilized. Not only could narratives create a shared organizational vision, they could also create new cultures, strategies, and even organizational identities. I would later apply what I learned at Second City to changing the death penalty process.

■ ■ ■

My broader ideas about change developed under several influences: academic, practical, and personal. Academically, I combined narrative theory with structuration theory,[2] which describes how we collectively produce the cognitive structures that then guide our actions, behavior, and interpretations. Our actions are never uninformed. We always use something to guide our actions and decisions, whether we are aware of it or not. I focused on how the ideas that we go by are produced, and how we can change our framework by changing our narrative, so new actions and understandings become possible. Eventually I developed the method I used to help design and organize the country's first permanent death penalty defense team.

Lots of research points out how we use structures, like maps, to guide us through social interactions. For example, most of us have some cognitive model, or structure, that represents what we expect to happen, and how we are supposed to act, during a job interview. When we "go by" that structure, we use our narrative of a job interview to guide us through the performance of a specific job interview, probably seeking information about the duties and expectations of the job while selling ourselves as a potential match for the position. We may act more professionally than we do among friends in informal social situations.

The job interview narrative is pretty widely shared, providing us with common norms and practices. The interviewer should not ask about age, race, or sexual orientation, and applicants should avoid politics and focus on job requirements and whether there is a match with our knowledge, ability, and skills. Both interviewer and applicant share elements across this shared narrative for how the interview should go and the kind of things that should or should not be said. Interviewee and interviewer are both enacting their narratives, which may entail separate roles for each of them but also contain shared understandings. Things go more smoothly when everyone sticks to the script.

Although there is wide agreement that these structures are part of our cognitive framework, far less research has focused on how these structures are created or changed. We know they guide us, but how do they get into our mental framework? And how do we create new ones—and make them stick? The death penalty team definitely did not want to go by the usual script, which was resulting in a large number of death sentences in Texas. We wanted to rewrite the script and change the norms of death penalty cases. It was this transformative agenda that led to my narrative change model.

Practically, I was informed by my experience at Second City. Instead of just studying narratives to make inferences about their meanings, I realized that narratives could be more purposefully and intentionally used to create, and then enact, new meanings and new social orders. New narratives could change the way people think and behave. Second City scripts were changing organizational cultures by literally proposing new narratives for how employees should act. This shift to creating meaning rather than just reflecting meaning was a new mindset theoretically as well.

Personally, new stories had saved my life. I was addicted to alcohol. After I got sober, I realized that examining the narratives I was going by had helped frame my recovery. I had been trapped in a horrible cycle of reenacting the same detrimental narrative, over and over, no matter what it cost me. I was a daily drinker, and when I drank, I could not stop. Many mornings I solemnly swore I would not drink that day, only to wind up passed out. I only drank when there was good news, or bad news, or if nothing happened. I drank if people wouldn't leave me alone, or if they did. In the end, I was nothing more than a drink in search of a reason. It was a deadly cycle. I thought I was a victim. I could not see that I was the architect of my own prison. Although I was sick and tired of being sick and tired, the plot never changed. I could not fathom a life without alcohol. Enacting a new narrative gave me a new way to live.

■ ■ ■

My narrative change model is illustrated in figure 3.1. This model should make intuitive sense given what I have said so far. We can all examine the narratives we go by in various areas of our lives and reflect on how they control us. We can question these narratives and endeavor to create and enact new narratives that bring different realities to fruition.

Starting at the top of what I call the narrative loop and moving counterclockwise, one of the central premises is that our lives are organized and guided by narratives. Narratives make up our

Figure 3.1 The narrative change model

Source: Figure by the author

cognitive frameworks; they are stories or assumptions we go by when behaving, acting, and making interpretations. Countless narratives reside in our cognitive frameworks, and we draw on them to guide us through any particular situation or interaction. Our actions are never unguided. Narratives provide shared social norms and conventions. You could say that a culture is a collection of narratives: stories about what is important to that society, such as how we value families or achievements or rugged individualism. Narratives pressure us to conform, and to the extent that our narratives are widely shared, other people have expectations about how we should behave in certain situations. Narratives vary in size and scope, from large narratives about marriage, parenthood, or even capitalism to small narratives about cueing in lines or where to face in an elevator. Whatever the scope of the narrative, it is active in guiding our everyday decisions and sensemaking. In figure 3.1, I depict narratives as being "over" us, guiding and controlling our actions, behaviors, and interpretations.

We encounter many kinds of narratives in our lives. Children's stories provide explicit rules, whereas the rules of dating are subtle and less formal. Most of us have been told about "the boy who cried wolf." The basic rule found in that narrative is "do not raise false alarms" because no one will come to your aid when you really do need help. More simply put: Don't lie.

Karma is a widely shared cultural story that people use as a guide for behavior and to explain events. The karma narrative tells us that events are connected by causation; what we do and what happens to us are closely related. When someone treats us poorly, we may believe that "they'll get theirs" at some time in the future. Events will eventually be evened out, and some punishment will balance the bad deed we experienced. Karma also influences how we should act. We may do good deeds expecting to be rewarded by karma; if we do good things, good things will in turn happen to us. When something unfortunate occurs, either we deserved it somehow or it will all balance out in the future. Karma incentivizes us to act well so that karma will bring fortuitous events into our lives. In fact, many cultures have narratives that align with the underlying logic that your actions play a large role in determining what happens to you. Few things are explained by chance. In the extreme, we could stick to this script to explain everything that happens to us.

The left side of the model in figure 3.1 shows that we are pressured to conform to the norms in the narrative. There is simultaneous guidance and pressure. Narratives provide the norms we should apply in navigating certain situations, and by conforming to those behavioral norms we are also controlled—pressured to act in socially prescribed ways.

We may not be conscious of the controlling narrative, but it provides us with deeply held, unquestioned ways of thinking and acting. We do not question our own actions; we just assume we are supposed to do things in a particular way. Although we are pressured to adhere to these norms, the narratives feel normal and natural to us. We take them for granted and believe we are making choices rather than being controlled. We assume the particular way in which we think is a universal truth. We often do things for no better reason than "that's the way it has always been done." Narratives, along with their rules and norms, can feel like impenetrable facts without origins. Our explanations are fragile but seemingly immutable: "That's just the way things are" or the completely indefensible yet unchallenged "It's always been that way, and always will be."

Let's turn to the right side of the model now to discover how narratives come into being. We construct narratives; they are socially constructed. We make them. We produce them. We build them. Narratives are not naturally occurring phenomena. We do not find them like we find objects and minerals in the earth. We create, share, and adopt them, and we are not always conscious of where we pick up these narratives. Although it may seem that "that's just the way things are," at least in the social world, things are only the way we make them.[3] When we objectify narratives, we seldom consider changing the way things are. We rarely stop to think about why we think the way we do.

The enactment side of the model shows that narratives emerge from our actions, behaviors, and interpretations as we make sense of events and come up with explanations or decide what to do in a situation. In describing what happened in any given situation, we produce a narrative. Anthropologists contend that narratives are the result of problem solving. When groups are faced with a problem, they resolve it by generating a narrative about "what to do" when faced with that situation in the future. As people enact this narrative when faced with the same problem, they reinforce the norms for what to do in that situation. This amounts to reproducing a narrative on the enactment side of the narrative loop: When that happens, we do this.

If the narrative is successful in navigating the situation, or solving a routine problem, we keep reproducing that narrative as long as it works. And sometimes, as you will see, we continue to reproduce and reenact narratives long after they have quit working. Texas continues to use the death penalty even though the costs are enormous and the payoff is a myth. In my own life, I enacted a narrative of addiction that was killing me. No cost was ever going to keep me from reproducing that narrative.

4
Applying the Model

When you go to one of the many Mexican restaurants in Texas, you are sure to be served chips and salsa as soon as you sit down. This is neither a law nor an industry regulation, but a Mexican restaurant that doesn't meet this widely and deeply shared customer expectation will find staying in business next to impossible. I don't think you'd last a week if you owned a Mexican restaurant that didn't serve free chips and salsa.

Norms are social expectations, things that we collectively agree on explicitly or implicitly. Some norms—like free chips and salsa at Mexican restaurants in Texas—achieve a status of being unquestioned. These norms are taken for granted, but there are dangers embedded in this acceptance. Narratives and the norms they contain don't have to be true for us to adhere to them. They are just the way things are done. For example, we don't consider strange cultural behaviors to be true or false; they are simply the way we do things around here, which can easily become the way things have *always* been done. We share as well as reify the cultural norms inherent in the logic of narratives that influence the way we act and make sense of events.

Unquestioned cultural assumptions often guide our actions and our decision-making.

■ ■ ■

There are many narratives in the legal world, and the practice of the law is, I am tempted to say, guided as much by norms as by legalities. In the death penalty, the way things are done is rife with powerful norms that people use without questioning them. For example, the following narrative is one of the most sacred principles of our justice system: People are innocent until proven guilty. I am confident that you have heard this line, and you have probably uttered it at one time or another. In death penalty trials, I have seen jurors solemnly claim that they can adhere to this principle of presumed innocence.

"They are innocent until proven guilty," a potential juror in Seth Rose's trial proudly announced with steadfast resolve. This person wanted to assure us that he or she had no biases regarding the case. As a legal principle, the presumption of innocence places the burden of proof on the prosecution. The widespread and unquestioned narrative, even spreading outside of the law and into mainstream U.S. culture, is that an individual is "innocent until proven guilty."

But that is not correct—it is not the actual legal phrase. The legal statute in Texas reads that jurors are to presume the defendant is "innocent *unless* proven guilty." *Unless* versus *until* turns out to make a huge difference. Going by a narrative that says innocent *until* proven guilty results in jurors unconsciously being guided to find the defendant guilty rather than innocent! The exact opposite of what the law intends. One little mistaken word turns this enduring principle completely upside down, and we don't even realize it. The word *until*, which almost all of us "go by," actually presumes that the defendant will *eventually* be found guilty, completely undermining the presumption of innocence on which our entire justice system rests. Guilt becomes a foregone conclusion instead of a presumption to be avoided. So if we go by our most widespread and strongly adhered to legal narrative, we unconsciously presume guilt rather than innocence. I cannot even fathom how much this misleading narrative has cost society. How many people has this narrative sent to prison? Or to death?

Remember that the power of a narrative is not related to its truthfulness. Power is a function of how controlling or widespread a narrative is—not how accurate it is. When we adopt a narrative without question, it is usually because we have been socialized to do so. The power of a narrative is more about the degree to which it guides behavior and how deeply it is embedded in our society. Powerful narratives become objectified and taken for granted.

Maybe you think this is merely semantics, that it is not consequential. What if you were on trial? Would you rather jurors were told a narrative that you are innocent *until* they find you guilty or that you are innocent *unless* they find you guilty? Which narrative presumes and retains innocence? Even if jurors are instructed with the correct legal text, it is highly likely that they will actually go by the popular, yet incorrect, narrative that says you are innocent *until* proven guilty. In the minds of jurors, that narrative unconsciously tips the scales of justice toward guilt. Up against this powerful narrative, the truth would scarcely set you free.

■ ■ ■

The death penalty institution had been relatively stable in Texas leading up to our narrative change intervention. Lots of pressures operated in death penalty cases, pushing everyone in the system toward executions. To provide a broader context for the changes our death penalty only team made, some background on this time is necessary.

The most relevant time period, legally and culturally, begins with reinstatement of the death penalty in the mid-1970s. Discussion of the broader historical context and some macro narratives that guided the operation of the death penalty at that time are useful in understanding what we were up against in changing the death penalty at the practice level. I discuss some macro narratives that played a role in our work transforming the death penalty, but the changes we enacted most successfully were at the practice level, in the capital murder trial process.

In 1972, the Supreme Court ruled that the death penalty was so arbitrary and capricious that it amounted to cruel and unusual punishment, a violation of the Eighth Amendment of the U.S. Constitution. At that time, Texas's death row held forty-five inmates, and all of their sentences were commuted to life in prison, emptying death row. Texas broke its back to write new death penalty statutes that would reinstate the death penalty. Attempting to set consistent criteria for charging people with the death penalty, states established a bifurcated trial, with one phase to determine guilt or innocence and another to determine a sentence. Death row got its first new resident in 1974, a month after reinstatement, and he hung himself. Texas had to wait until 1982 to carry out its first execution since reinstatement. Since then, the State of Texas has executed more than five hundred people.

Executions increased throughout the 1990s and continued at a good pace into the 2000s. I had only been at Texas Tech for a few months on that fateful day when my phone rang with a call from Michael Block, but Texas had already carried out twenty-six executions that year.

The death penalty is supposed to be about justice, but that value is easily eclipsed by the three most significant factors determining who gets death: race, money, and politics. The death penalty is worse than arbitrary; it is rife with biases. The death penalty is supposedly reserved for the worst of the worst, which is supposed to be determined by considering *aggravating circumstances* related to a murder or murders. When deciding whether or not to seek the death penalty, aggravating factors include things like the age of the victim. If the victim is six years old or younger (this has recently been raised to ten years old), then the murder is a capital offense. Murder during the commission of a robbery, for instance, brought James Neely's charges up from murder to capital murder.

The list of aggravators has continued to grow, expanding the offenses eligible for capital punishment. But, in reality, whether or not someone gets the death penalty does not depend on any aspect of the crime itself as much as it does on race. Race is by far the most common determinant of whether someone is charged with the death penalty. Perhaps counterintuitively, the most important factor is the race of the victim, followed by the race of the defendant. Although the heinousness of the murder is supposed to be a factor, it appears that there is nothing more heinous in Texas than minorities killing white people.

Two implicit racist narratives are still active in the death penalty context. Even a cursory look at death row statistics will tell you that as a society we still go by these narratives. One narrative says that minorities are more dangerous and thus more deserving of death. Another narrative says that murdering a white person is worse than murdering a black person. It is only the naïve who are surprised to find that racist narrative in our justice system.

In *The Behavior of Law*, Donald Black describes how sociological factors, not legal factors, influence the justice system.[1]

Black points out that the practice of law on the ground, in the streets and courtrooms, can be very different from the law on the books. We do not always practice what we preach. Justice is guided by norms just as much as laws, and those norms promulgate inequality based on social status. Given our country's history and present, social status is still closely intertwined with race.

Black explains how the law generates different amounts of force based on differences in the socioeconomic status between victim and offender. When the victim has high social status and the offender has low social status, more punishment is brought to bear on the offender. When the maid slaps a rich housewife, the maid goes to jail. When the housewife slaps the maid, nothing happens. The assault has less impact on what happens legally than on the differences in social status between the parties involved. Social status is the most significant determinant of the amount of punishment or how much law is brought to bear in resolving the situation. When a black person kills a white person, the black person gets the death penalty. When a white person kills a black person . . . well . . . let's look at some numbers.

The Supreme Court considered a case that cited an empirical study showing that defendants with white victims were 4.3 times more likely to receive the death penalty. In Texas, if you are black and kill someone white, all else being equal, you are 22 times more likely to receive the death penalty than if you are white and kill someone who is black. On Texas's death row, 70 percent of the inmates had white victims, and only 11 percent had black victims. Combined, this means that less than 1 percent of death row inmates are white people who killed black people. Most people go to death row for killing white people, very few for killing black people, and almost no whites go to death row for killing black people.[2]

It is not that more whites are killed than blacks. More than half of U.S. murder victims are black, and they are 4 times more likely to be murdered than whites. Rather, it is that more justice is sought and more law is brought to bear when whites are killed.

"Justice is blind" is another narrative we preach more often than practice in the justice system. Many courthouses are adorned with Lady Justice statues. She is holding balanced scales of justice and wearing a blindfold, illustrating that the law is fair and balanced and everyone is treated equally. Perhaps Lady Justice cannot see race, but when we apply the law, Lady Justice loves to peek, and the first thing she notices is skin color. If you are black, she drops the scales and draws her sword.

Race, a supposedly impermissible factor in the justice system, turns out to be *the only predictable criterion* in determining who gets the death penalty. The death penalty isn't arbitrary, it's worse—it is selectively based on race. As a society, our actions are speaking loud and clear, and they are saying uncomfortable things. In Texas, we use the death penalty to kill minorities who kill white people. In actual practice of the law, being black or Hispanic is an aggravating circumstance.

Help is not on the way. The Supreme Court cannot do anything about racism in the system as a whole. They can only rule on individual cases. The disproportionate number of minorities on death row is not something the Supreme Court can address. Any attempt to correct the effects of the death penalty system is simply a band-aid. Wiping away the footprints of the monster does nothing to the monster itself. Perhaps we turn to the courts to decide the fate of the death penalty because courts have done so before, but getting rid of the death penalty will take legislation and a vote. Society must decide. Public support for the death penalty, although at a forty-year low, is still in the majority. Either we don't understand what we are supporting, or worse, we don't care.

Understanding the societal narratives that guide the death penalty are important because those narratives are manifested at the practice level—actions that result in putting people to death. Understanding the exorbitant narrative pressures the death penalty team was up against helped us strategize when creating narratives at the practice level. I had little hope of changing societal level narratives related to the death penalty as an institution, but understanding the narratives of people in our own death penalty context at the street level was helpful. We knew what we were up against in achieving our goal, which was to save one life. And then the next. And so on.

Focusing on narratives that guided the death penalty process at the practice level left plenty for us to attempt to change, and we intended to do so dramatically. For example, another reason for the lopsided racial proportions on death row was that the poor do not receive good legal representation. This we could change. In doing so, we might also affect some of the macro narratives, such as money and politics, that direct who gets death. We made changes at the practice level that recognized and resisted institutional pressures related to money and politics. We could not change the rules of the game, but we could change how we played the game.

In the death penalty game, the playing field is not equal. The rules are biased toward the prosecution and tip the scales toward death, which is evident in the overwhelming results—Texas offenders were subject to the death penalty more than 90 percent of the time in capital trials. Some of this is related to legalities, but just as often the results stem from enactment of powerful cultural narratives that contain damaging norms. In our change model, we recognized those narrative pressures and implemented ways to resist them. We did not have to keep doing things the way they had always been done. One example is how we engaged in courtroom objections. It may seem like a small thing, but the implications were surprising. In court, whenever there is an objection or a motion, the judge must rule on it. You have probably seen this on TV.

"Objection!" an attorney may say.

"Overruled," the judge may say and tap the gavel. The trial then proceeds with hardly any interruption at all.

This scene may be familiar to everyone, but most of us know little about the rules and norms that govern these complex exchanges. There is a lot going on under the surface of an objection.

Objection rules favor the prosecution. When the defense objects, they are required to provide a legal rationale for the objection, even if it is only a phrase indicating a rationale, such as "leading the witness" or even just the keyword "leading!" to indicate the prosecuting attorney is leading the witness to answer questions in certain ways. A single word is common for routine objections, even though the word references complex legal rules that are documented in case citations. If the defense has a more complex objection, perhaps based on constitutional grounds, they have to provide a detailed legal rationale for the objection and cite relevant case law when raising the objection. When the prosecution objects, however, they do not have to provide any rationale or cite any case law. In fact, the judge is directed to *automatically* "sustain" the prosecution's objections if the judge can contemplate—yes, merely contemplate—that some legal rationale *must* exist, even if the judge cannot cite it.

If you look over trial records and trial transcriptions, the favoritism offered to the prosecution is clear. If the defense objects, they have to cite a legal reason, whereas the prosecution only has to object and can presume that some legal reason must exist. Looking at objections in the trial transcript, you will see, time and time again, judges ruling in favor of the prosecution and against the defense, as a default. And the rules support this bias. Appellant attorneys have told me that reviewing the court record is like seeing the judge tick the prosecution box for the duration of a trial.

"Objection-sustained. Objection-sustained. Objection-sustained," one attorney described how reviewing prosecution objections looked. "But when it comes to the defense, it goes objection-overruled, objection-overruled, objection-overruled. And, there is never any indication as to why. Page after page, over the course of an entire trial, you can see judges ruling for the state. They are on automatic pilot."

This tiny narrative has major impacts. Every death penalty verdict automatically goes through an appeals process. On direct appeal, every judicial decision made during the trial is reviewed: whether or not an expert witness was allowed to testify, or whether an attorney could introduce some piece of evidence. As a general rule, if an issue was not raised during a trial, it cannot be raised on appeal. The logic is that courts don't want new issues raised at the appellate stage if they could have been addressed at the trial level. They might say, "If you did not think it was an issue then, why raise it now, after the fact?" I appreciate the logic. It is "speak now or forever hold your peace."

If you couple the rule that you cannot appeal an issue unless you raise it during trial with the rule that judges do not have to provide a legal rationale for their rulings, the effects can be doubly devastating for the defense. The problem is with one subtle norm in particular, and changing it requires a cultural change rather than a legal change.

If the judge simply says "Overruled," without providing a legal rationale, an appellate court cannot review the decision because no rationale is visible in the court record. So there is, in effect, nothing present to appeal. Appellate courts cannot project what the trial judge was thinking when he or she overruled an objection, so they presume, by default, that the implicit rationale must have been legitimate. Absent any legal rationale, the appeals court essentially refuses to project one, in effect saying, "We don't know why the judge ruled the way she or he did, so we can't overrule the decision." The result is that fewer decisions are reviewed, fewer errors are found, more convictions and punishments are upheld, fewer retrials are awarded, and more people die.

However, there is a legal rule that says an attorney can demand a written explanation for each and every ruling by the judge. This written explanation must then be entered into the formal court record, which makes the legal rationale explicitly present and available for review by appellate courts. Although you are allowed to ask the judge for a written ruling on every motion and objection, in practice this is just not done. There are strong norms against using this rule in the courtroom. In this instance, the narrative norm is much stronger than the courtroom legal rule. In your own organization, you can probably think of many examples where the official rules are trumped by even stronger norms.

This is a good place to note that it is necessary to understand the narratives you hold when attempting change. Part of our challenge in changing the way things are done was to be reflexive, to become aware of any constraining narratives that we were going by as a defense team. In the practice of death penalty defense, we had to be aware of, and be careful not to reenact, narratives that were detrimental to our goals. In changing the death penalty process, the narratives we did not enact were as important as the new ones we did enact.

For example, the culture in courtrooms calls for showing extreme deference to judges. Yes, attorneys should respect the judge and maintain courtroom decorum, but a larger incentive for showing extreme deference is because attorneys are dependent on judges for their livelihood. Attorneys who don't conform to these norms suffer financially. If court-appointed attorneys don't kowtow to judges, they find themselves appointed to fewer and fewer cases. People who buck the norms are blackballed, their income suffers, and eventually their career suffers. One effect of this narrative of deference is that defense attorneys are socialized not to request written rulings because it is a nuisance for the judge and may make the judge mad, eventually affecting the defense attorney's career.

Showing extreme deference to judges is a widespread narrative in the justice system, and not asking for written rulings is just one small outcome. Defense attorneys may enact this powerful and impactful narrative instead of doing what otherwise may save their client's life. They don't want to bother the judge with funding motions, requests for experts, objections, etc. This indoctrination starts formally in law school, yet even as children we are taught to show deference to those in authority. Yes, attorneys should respect the judge—but they should not be deferential to the judge at the expense of their clients.

I am often on the faculty for capital training seminars and breakout seminars in which we work real cases and brainstorm tactics the lawyers might use. In one session, I suggested that a lawyer file several funding requests for expert witnesses.

"The judge won't let me do that," the defense attorney said. He had also skipped several promising avenues toward receiving a plea offer because he suspected the judge would not approve—so he never asked.

"What do you mean, 'He won't let you?' " I demanded. I felt my face get hot. "The Constitution *lets you*. The judge doesn't get to decide that, the Constitution does, and the judge gets to uphold it." My rant was not so much to chide him as it was to inspire several other attorneys in the room who were just starting their first death penalty cases.

That attorney had adopted a very controlling narrative without reflecting on its impact. That narrative has a lot of legitimacy in Texas, where judges often vocalize a "this is MY courtroom" attitude and meet any dissent with hostility. Also, to be fair, attorneys are thinking about their careers. If they piss off the judge, they are unlikely to receive court appointments in the future. Their livelihood depends on showing extreme deference.

In addition to the power inequities, the judge is often a former prosecutor, and ruling against the defendant is a default position. After being told no enough times, a defense attorney may quit filing motions that have only a slight chance of benefiting the client but a big chance of drawing the judge's ire. In death penalty defense cases, all we get are slim chances, so we need all the chances we can muster, no matter who it may piss off. You cannot know which one of the slim chances may eventually save your client's life, so you have to take them all. Our team decided that we would be respectful, but we would use every tool at our disposal to save our clients' lives. In death penalty cases, someone's life is on the line, and going along to get along could result in the client's death. Before we enacted our own narratives with new norms and a new way of doing things, we had to be conscious of the norms that pressured us to act in certain ways.

One simple change in our narrative was beginning the courtroom practice of requesting written rulings on every motion and objection. It seems small, but this one tiny practice gave us two chances to save our client's life. Additional benefits were realized as well. Because the judge knew that the rulings would be reviewed, the judge quit automatically ruling for the prosecution every time. Judges still mainly ruled for the prosecution, but at least we got them off autopilot. They knew we were going to force them to explain themselves, a departure from current practice, so they had to be more considerate in their rulings.

Second, and more important, we did what death penalty attorneys call "perfect the record." We made every legal rationale "visible" and available for appellate courts to reconsider. More written rulings gave us more chances that an appellate court would find an error of judgment in a ruling. In reviewing the legal rationale behind the ruling, the appellate court might find fault with the judge's decision and award our client a retrial. It's a true lifeline.

Judges are elected. They are there because they won a popularity contest, not an intelligence contest. Our new practice of always requesting a written ruling was both a form of resistance to the current norms and an enactment of our new narrative that changed the way things are done. The request for a written ruling is done by invoking the rule of appellate procedure 33.1 (a)(2) (A) of the Texas Code of Criminal Procedure. We knew judges would not like it. We didn't care. Some would not like it because their decisions would be reviewed and their legal rationales would be under scrutiny. Requesting a written ruling is not just a nuisance; it could expose a judge's lack of legal knowledge. As Michael likes to say, "Not only do some Texas judges not know the law, they aren't even curious!"

"Judges may not like you," Michael said in a training seminar once, "but they will respect you. Make them write it down. It is not their choice. You have a right to request a written ruling every time. Do it every time. If they don't know the law, they will get an education."

I want to emphasize that we don't invoke this rule to make judges mad—we do it to save our client's life, even after it is out of our hands. When you request a written ruling, trial can proceed, but the judge will have to spend the evening writing out the legal rationales and putting them into the court record. He or she may have to look up case law. Good. They may not like the extra effort we require, but they may begin to think about their rulings more. The trial will become fairer once judges start to respect, rather than dismiss, our motions and objections.

When we enacted our "perfect the record" narrative and made sure the legal rationale underlying every decision was available for review, it gave the defendant another chance, however slim. Previously, the trial record would read:

PROSECUTION: "Objection."
JUDGE: "Sustained."

In reviewing this, an appellate court could take no action. They can't overturn decisions they cannot see in writing. They presumed that the judge's unspoken rationale was correct.

As a result of our new practice, we would force the judge to generate a written ruling and legal basis, which then must be entered into the official court record, which would now read:

STATE: "Objection."
JUDGE: "Sustained."
DEFENSE: "Your honor, we request a written ruling under appellate procedure 33.1."

The judge then had to write legal arguments to support the ruling and enter it into the court record. This ruling could be reviewed by higher courts. If the legal rationale was problematic, or the wrong case law was cited, the ruling could be overturned by higher courts. It could result in a retrial. It's not much of a shot in Texas, but it's one the client did not have before our new narrative.

The second chance to save our client's life that perfecting the record gave us is independent of the direct appeal of our own trial; it is related to other, future Supreme Court rulings. For example, in James Neely's trial, we enacted our perfect the record narrative to make sure every decision was available for review. If we filed a motion, we knew the judge would deny it, but we didn't care, we still filed it. It might not be a review of his own case that gives James Neely another chance. It could be another case, in another state even, where they find, for example, that some jury instruction is unconstitutional.

If the Supreme Court does rule that some jury instruction is unconstitutional, then any case where there was an objection or motion to find that same instruction unconstitutional will also be granted relief. If you don't file a motion, or object, the Supreme Court ruling does not apply to your client. You would have had to raise the same issue in your trial for the ruling to apply to your case. So we raised every issue we could think of, regardless of how the judge would rule. We were not really filing motions for our judge to rule on. We were filing motions for the Supreme Court to rule on. Maybe one day the Supreme Court will review the same issue on another case, and find in that person's favor—and retroactively, in our favor too.

Requesting a written ruling is one example of the many tiny narratives our team was devoted to enacting. As you can see, even the smallest changes can result in dramatic new outcomes. Given the historical results, we weren't really interested in the way things had always been done. We were up against some very powerful and controlling narratives, unquestioned narratives that unconsciously guided judges, prosecutors, jurors, defendants, and defense attorneys. In attempting to create and enact new narratives, we faced an uphill battle. I've heard defense lawyers characterize the unfairness and biases inherent in death penalty cases this way, "They get to push a boulder down a hill, and we get to try and stop it."

We wanted to stop enacting narratives that were detrimental to us. Being reflexive about the existing narratives and resisting them were as important for change as enacting the new narratives we created. We had to pay attention to both sides of the narrative change model simultaneously.

■ ■ ■

In your organization, you will certainly have to resist existing narratives in the course of enacting new ones. Your organization may introduce changes that go against long-standing industry norms. If you are reflexive, I am confident that you will become more conscious of the implicit narratives you enact even though they are detrimental to you. I would bet quite a bit of money that you are going by narratives that are not to your benefit, and you are probably not conscious of them. Most of us are not.

Picture everyone, including yourself, being pressured by narratives. We are all on automatic pilot most of the time. Being more reflexive will help you understand your own and others' behavior. It will convince you that you can enact new narratives to legitimate new behaviors. If you continue to enact the old narratives, you will remain stuck in the same old ways.

5
The Narrative Stranglehold

It was Susan Fowler's first day on her new team at Uber. She was so proud and happy to have landed a job as an engineer at a prestigious company. She loved it. Her new manager sent her a message over the company's chat system to welcome her aboard. Susan thanked him.

The manager quickly mentioned that he was in an open relationship. Soon he confided that both he and his girlfriend were free to have sex with other people; his girlfriend was getting laid all the time, but he was not having any luck. The manager said he knew he should not be looking to hook up at work, but he was desperate for someone to have sex with him.

Susan was shocked. "How stupid can this guy be?" she wondered. She took screen shots of the chat and reported him to human resources immediately. She imagined fast action.

Human resource executives at Uber eventually got back to Susan Fowler about her sexual harassment complaint. They recognized that sexual harassment had occurred and promised that change was on the way.

Unfortunately, it was Susan who would have to do all the changing. Susan had picked her department because it matched her interests, expertise, and experience. She was told by HR that she could move to another team. It was more than a suggestion. If she did not move, she was told she could expect a negative performance review. They added that if Susan did not drop this and move, she was asking for retaliation.

As to why her manager did not face any consequences, HR claimed it was his first offense and that he should only get a warning. As a further rationale for why he should not be punished, upper management added that he was a very high performer.

It is the law that people who report harassment cannot have their positions or work duties changed as a result. We do not want victims to face retaliation for speaking out. Management knew it would have to look like Susan wanted to change positions within the company, and they pressured her to say it was her idea to request a transfer.

Susan resisted the Hobson's choice presented to her and took her complaint higher up the chain of command. She was met with even stronger sentiments of the same type: Susan needed fixing, not Uber. The $100-billion-dollar ride-share company knew that moving Susan would not fix the problem. They were entirely uninterested in fixing the problem. They wanted to protect their high performers, no matter the cost.

Narratives at Uber created and supported this culture. Uber had a "bro culture" that was insular and competitive at the same time. Travis Kalanick, the founder and CEO, fostered this ethos. Stories at Uber gave accolades to cutthroat competiveness and made "bad boy" behavior and displays of sexual prowess seem heroic. The narratives of what was considered cool at Uber— behaving badly and undercutting others to meet goals—became signs of achievement.

Kalanick loved that the company culture revolved around him and that it was the kind of culture he had been excluded from in high school and college. By authoring this damaging narrative

at Uber, Kalanick had finally found a way to be a cultural icon.
Many of us were brought up in environments like this. I work
on a college campus, and it is hard to miss that binge drinking is
part of a regressive competitive male culture, where how much
you can drink, or how many sexual partners you have, becomes
a status symbol. That philosophy was flourishing at Uber, and to
flourish it had to have lots of support.

What Uber needed most from Susan was for her to conform
to the company norms.

■ ■ ■

We are conformists—most of the time. We conform to social
norms to fit in, sometimes under some pretty strong pressure.
When I was a kid in grade school, there was a particular brand of
shoe that was the "in" shoe for kids. I had the more economical
knock-offs. Everyone at school spotted the difference right away
and ridiculed me because I did not adhere to the norm. Embarrassed, I refused to wear the shoes again. That experience was a
lesson in how social pressure to conform to norms works, and
what happens if you don't follow the crowd.

Organizations are not much different. We might like to think
that organizations prioritize things in the interest of efficiency
and effectiveness, but many times they are simply conforming
to norms or social expectations. Remember my Mexican restaurant example? Serving free chips and salsa is a norm in that
institutionalized field based on social expectations. If Mexican
restaurants don't conform to this ideal, people will see them as
illegitimate. Institutional theorists have painted the most complete picture of this conformity.[1] They say that organizations
conform to social expectations to attain legitimacy, which is
conferred upon them by others in the institutional environment.

If organizations are not seen as legitimate, resources will eventually stop flowing their way, and they will cease to exist. So organizations conform to norms in order to survive.

Corporations do not do things for irrational reasons—it is natural to want to fit in by conforming to norms. However, those norms are made up. They are social conventions created by people, and organizations adhere to these socially constructed norms in the face of some very strong pressures and penalties for not conforming. Narratives and institutional theory are intertwined because these narratives become institutionalized so the norms are not questioned. Narratives become "the way things have always been," even if they are quite new.

This book is about creating and enacting new narratives. You can also think of it as bringing visions to fruition, or turning ideas into reality. This type of change work requires that we understand exactly *how* things like norms come to be. The field of ethnomethodology[2] is distinguished by a focus on how these processes occur—or in our case, how narratives become enacted and accepted. Ethnomethodology closely examines the processes by which narratives are created, how norms become established, and how they become institutionalized. The leap to creating new norms then only requires us to apply our theoretical understanding of these processes.

Let's take an illustration from my own university to understand how something becomes institutionalized. At Texas Tech we have a fabulous recreation center. The Texas Tech Recreation Center receives a lot of accolades for having the best extras, including yoga and dozens of other fitness classes, saunas, and massages. You can rent bikes, camping equipment, and ski gear. There is a huge rock wall and athletic courts of every type. However, at the top of the amenities list may be our leisure pool, which has been voted among the best for a university. The leisure pool area includes wet and dry sundecks, a beach slope entry, and a long lazy river encircling the whole complex, complete with inner tubes to idly float on the river. It feels like an expensive luxury resort.

The question is, "Why does a university, an institution of higher learning, have a leisure pool?" How did it come to be? What process resulted in our having a leisure pool? Does it make the university more efficient? More effective? Our mission statement talks about advancing knowledge through teaching, research, and scholarship. It talks about students becoming ethical global leaders. Having the world's greatest leisure pool does not help us fulfill that mission, nor does it make us more efficient or effective. In fact, the leisure pool is completely unrelated to our mission.

Gyms, courts, and sports fields have been on campuses for quite a while, but formal stand-alone recreation centers only began to emerge in the 1980s. It was not long before nice recreation facilities became a widely held expectation among students. Universities had to quickly follow this norm if they hoped to retain their legitimacy and long-term survival. Our leisure pool serves no purpose other than to make us look cool (or legitimate) to current and future students. Truth be told, being accepted by stakeholders is a crucial aim for every institution. Our prospective students (aka customers) want cool leisure pools on their campus, and having these facilities has become a strong social expectation that having them ensures we are deemed "legit" by our stakeholders. Although it does not make the university more efficient or effective, it helps the university survive. A university without terrific recreational facilities is like a Mexican restaurant without chips and salsa. These things are done, these expectations are met, to secure our continued existence. And, yes, it also means we are conformists.

The severe pressure to adhere to norms is one of the most difficult hurdles to overcome in transformational change, but it is an aspect of change that existing models don't address.[3] Powerful norms, made even more insidious when they are unquestioned, are among the most substantial challenges we face in creating change. Going against the norm is a monumental task, and it has nothing to do with seeking efficiency, building a more effective mousetrap, or finding a rational explanation. New narratives must fight for legitimacy. The most difficult part of change is creating and enacting a new narrative and achieving space inside people's cognitive and normative frameworks.

When enacting a new narrative, we may be going against institutionalized norms and bucking strong social expectations. Narratives entail norms applicable to particular situations, and any new norms will struggle to attain legitimacy. If we do not enact the right narrative, other people will deem our actions illegitimate. In trying to establish new social expectations, we are going against existing expectations. Later, in exploring how we might increase the chances that our new narrative will become accepted and institutionalized, I discuss several strategies that can help a new narrative attain legitimacy.

In the meantime, we are supposed to stick to the script and align ourselves with the dominant conventional wisdom. Indeed, others will almost certainly challenge the legitimacy of the new narrative. All sorts of pressures will constrain our actions and behaviors as we try to introduce a new narrative. Change may call for rebellion, and people reenacting the same old narratives will not appreciate rebellion, especially those who benefit from how it always has been done.

What are we up against when we attack existing narratives? Most of the time we go through life on autopilot, reenacting narratives labeled *reconstructive action loops* (see figure 5.1).

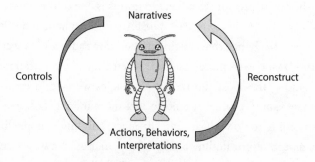

Figure 5.1 Reconstruction action loops

Source: Figure by the author

Remember that the left side of the narrative change model illustrates how we are guided and controlled by narratives. In reconstructive action loops, we simply reconstruct a behavior, which becomes even more institutionalized. You might say that the norms become stronger and stronger every time we go by them. A reconstructive loop maintains the status quo. Because we often take these narratives for granted, we do not question how they direct us to behave.

Reproducing the current narrative takes little intention or effort. We are in this mode most of the time in our daily lives—it is how we sail smoothly through our day. It makes for consistency, which is not necessarily a bad thing, like taking the same route to work every day. We use the same narratives in our social interactions and adhere to the same norms. For example, when we return items at retail stores, we all know the script and what to expect. Who has time to treat every return like it is the first time it ever happened? We enact many narratives on a daily basis to script us through routine practices— oil changes, haircuts, speeding tickets—and that was just my morning! Going by existing narratives eases social interaction, and things go smoothly for you. Behave according to social expectations and you will fit in. Others will accept you and your actions.

■ ■ ■

In the death penalty setting, I encountered several controlling narratives that were deadly, one of which was the "10-2 rule." A death penalty trial has two phases: trial and sentencing. If the defendant is found guilty at the end of the trial, only then does the jury move to the second phase, or sentencing hearing. It is in this second phase that the jury decides whether to hand down a life or a death sentence. During the sentencing hearing, the jury considers mitigating and aggravating evidence. Just as in a trial, witnesses are called and experts testify. After hearing all the evidence, the jury will once again be asked to deliberate. They answer two questions, literally ticking boxes. The 10-2 rule is a formal narrative embedded in a statute in Texas that applies to these death penalty deliberations.

These two questions appeared on the verdict sheet on the jury charge in James Neely's trial:

Question 1: Do you find from evidence beyond a reasonable doubt that there is a probability that the Defendant would commit criminal acts of violence that constitute a continuing threat to society?

Question 2: Are you convinced that there is no mitigating circumstance that would warrant a sentence of less than death?

Jurors are further instructed,

The first question must be answered "yes" unanimously or "no" by a vote of at least ten-to-two. The second question must be answered "no" unanimously or "yes" by a vote of at least ten-to-two.

All twelve jurors must answer unanimously on both questions to deliver a death sentence. Any other combination automatically results in a sentence of life without parole. If they don't all agree on the first question, they don't even move on to consider the second question.

The first question is referred to as the "future danger" question. If the defendant is deemed not to be of any danger in the future, there is no need to kill him. Only if the jury unanimously agrees "yes" on the future danger question—the defendant will commit criminal acts of violence in the future—do they move on to the second question. This question asks jurors whether any mitigating circumstance, such as mental illness, would warrant a sentence of less than death. If they unanimously agree "no" on this question, the judge, by mandate, orders a death sentence.

Our justice system, and society as a whole, prefers that the entire jury agrees on a sentence. We don't want any doubt, and we don't want to go by a simple majority in such a grave matter. However, the court also wants a preponderance of agreement for life, and it instructs the jury that they need at least ten jurors to deliver a life sentence.

What is the problem with this? The jury is misled by the instructions. In actuality, it only takes one juror, not ten, to deliver a life sentence. The judge is mandated to enter a life sentence on anything less than unanimous agreement on death. But no one tells the jury how the process really works. In fact, no one is allowed to! Texas statute orders that the jury cannot be informed of the result of a verdict that is not unanimous. They are left wondering what happens when they are in a so-called deadlock, and juries often draw their own misinformed conclusions.

You should not be surprised to hear that their actions are dictated by powerful and controlling—inaccurate—narratives. As you will recall, accuracy has little to do with whether or not we embrace a narrative. In fact, juries usually fail to agree on a sentence on their first round of voting. They may be split at 6 to 6, or 5 for life and 7 for death, or any combination less than 12 to 0 for death and at least 10 to 2 for life. When the jury is deadlocked and cannot tick either box, they are instructed to inform the judge. But the judge cannot help. He or she will merely request that the jury continue to deliberate in an attempt to reach agreement.

The judge's response never offers any clarification, and the jury assumes the judge is implying that they must reach an agreement. If they don't, they assume they will be considered a "hung jury." But unlike the trial phase, there is no such thing as a hung jury in a sentencing hearing. If they fail to agree on a sentence, by default, the judge must enter a life sentence. Even if there is a sole holdout, and the vote is 11 to 1 for death, the judge must enter a life sentence.

Because no one can tell the jury how it really works, the jurors go by existing narratives in their cognitive frameworks. They get these ideas from TV. If a jury is deadlocked, the jurors believe that the defendant will be declared "free to go." You can imagine how the jurors must feel when they cannot all agree to kill someone. They have just agreed that the defendant is guilty of murder in the trial phase. If they do not reach an agreement to deliver a death sentence now, they falsely believe that the defendant may be set free.

I saw these narratives at work in gut-wrenching fashion during the Seth Rose trial. I sat in on jury selection when a group of about fifty potential jurors were being qualified. During jury qualification, the prosecutor and defense explain to the jury how deliberations work to the extent they are legally allowed to do so. This is one of the times when jurors may be dismissed; the other is during individual juror questioning, or voir dire. For example, a simple reason to dismiss a potential juror from serving on a capital murder trial is a weak stomach. Attorneys from both sides tell jurors they will be seeing some disturbing crime scene photos. They ask for a show of hands of whether jurors think they may have nightmares or be emotionally disturbed. Some people are understandably squeamish.

"I'll faint," says one that day.

"Can you elaborate?" asks the prosecutor.

"If I see blood or anything like that, I'll literally faint."

"Even in photos?" the defense attorney asks.

"Yes, sir. Even saying the word blood just now is making me feel sick."

The juror is dismissed, and the judge thanks the person for his or her service.

Later that same day the prosecutor finishes explaining the two questions potential jury members would be asked to answer during sentencing deliberations, correctly reminding them that they only get to that point if the defendant is found guilty during the first phase. The prosecutor asks if anyone has any questions about how the process works.

A woman raises her hand. She motioned to one of the defense attorneys. "What happens to him if we don't *all* vote for death?" Many of the potential jurors nod; they have the same question.

As I have said, the real answer is that a sentence of life without parole must automatically be entered by the judge. The trial will be concluded. But because of the Texas statute, no one can tell the jury the whole truth and nothing but the truth.

"The judge will tell you what he can when we get there," says the defense attorney.

"Well . . . does he go free?" she asks frantically.

Just as research has shown,[4] jurors assume they will be declared a hung jury, or worse, that the defendant will be acquitted and the judge will announce that he is free to go. The truth is, however, once found guilty of murder in the trial phase, the punishment is life without parole by default. Nothing can change that. It is the minimum sentence for capital murder. In the sentencing phase, the jury is really only deciding whether to increase the sentence to death. If they fail to agree, the default is life.

"I am not allowed to answer that," the attorney says, "but like I said, the judge will instruct you if and when we get to that point."

In fact, the jury will never get an answer to that question. The judge will merely refer them to the jury charge with the two questions but never provide guidance about what happens if the jurors don't agree on a sentence. It is illegal to tell them. Texas likes that jurors don't know. They know being misinformed leads to more death sentences.

The second narrative that works in combination with the 10-2 rule to control the jury is one you will be familiar with: the majority rules. *Majority rules* is a common narrative that most of us have gone by at one time or another. It says that we all get a vote, and whatever option the majority votes for, the entire group will ascribe to that decision. Perhaps you have decided where to eat by taking a vote among a group of friends: Who wants Chinese, raise your hand? Who wants Mexican?

You can see how powerful these narratives are at controlling actions. When the jurors assume a mistrial or worse if they don't all agree, they do just what you would expect if you were in the same situation—they reach an agreement using the norm majority rules. Holdouts in sentencing deliberations usually cave under the pressure to conform to this narrative and join those voting for death. Who wants life? Who wants death?

In 278 death sentences given nationwide, the Capital Jury Research Project found that the jury was *not* unanimously for death during the first vote in the jury room in 275 cases.

Although the jury had not reached an agreement at the first vote, all of them eventually arrived at a unanimous death sentence. The lifers caved every time. The narrative pressure to kill is nearly insurmountable.

Our team fought narratives at all levels. Aside from the justice system itself, we had to resist practice level narratives on the defense team. To save our clients' lives, we had to build trust— but some narratives were undermining that goal.

Society does not hold public defenders in high regard because they see them as getting dangerous criminals off and putting them on the streets again. Defendants do not think much of public defenders either. Public defenders are, after all, "free" for those who cannot afford an attorney, and defendants think you get what you pay for. Defendants also presume that public defenders do not really care what happens to them, and that they don't try very hard to defend them. Or worse, defendants think public defenders assume they are guilty and may even be working against them. Because we are being paid by the state, defendants think we will do what the state wants. It is a rational assumption.

"You get paid by the state don't you?" clients say.

"Yes," we say.

"Then you're working for them, not me. I certainly can't pay no lawyer. They payin' you, you gonna do what they want you to do." Even when we manage, by Herculean efforts, to get plea bargains that save their lives, defendants still suspect we are working with the DA to put them away forever. This lack of trust becomes an impediment to helping them.

All of our clients are poor, and they have not had many positive experiences with any public services, much less with law enforcement. As children, they may have been put into foster care by a social service that they saw as taking away their parents.

Their past experiences with state institutions are likely to have seared distrust into their perceptions. If they are on welfare, people accuse them of being freeloaders. People ridicule them. Any help they have gotten in the past has come with stigmatism. This distrust in the immediate foreground is set against a backdrop of an entire legal system rigged against poor clients. They think the state is "out to get them," and it is hard to say they are entirely wrong.

Finally, our clients are not stalwarts for taking responsibility. Like all of us, they are flawed and have character defects. As a result of all these factors, our first client meetings are often with people who think nothing is their fault, that the entire system is rigged against them, and that we are either in on it or don't care. That's a hard place to start.

"We're not like that," we tell them. "We would not be here if the State of Texas was not serious about killing you. Our goal is to save your life." We try to explain how our office works and the new system. Unlike public defenders they may have had in the past, we are not doing anything but death penalty cases. No one in the office is struggling to run a private practice or giving paying clients priority over court appointed clients. We are also honest about their situation.

Part of our new narrative is to do something for them immediately following that first meeting. Perhaps they ask us to call their mom, get them some reading material, or get them moved voluntarily to administrative segregation because they are having interpersonal problems with their cell mates. This is especially important if we suspect there are jailhouse snitches who will claim our client confessed. Following through for our client begins the long process of building trust.

Many eventually trust us. After several months, they see fewer and fewer of their friends, maybe even their family, which can be quite dysfunctional. These defendants did not have the best of lives and relationships to begin with, and by the time they are facing the death penalty, they often have absolutely no one left. They certainly have no one to speak for them, except us. Their anger may be directed at us, but we still come. Our mitigators spend countless hours building a relationship and hearing about their life story. The attorneys always respond to questions quickly and try to meet weekly. We are trying to understand our clients, not judge them, and we are straightforward about what is happening on their case. This devotion and attention, just being there, builds trust. They are often hesitant to tell their life stories, as most have dark pasts.

"Their deepest, darkest secret, that one thing they don't want to tell anyone, or the thing they've never told anyone," a mitigator told me once, "that's what I need them to tell me. The one thing they don't want anybody to know is probably the one thing that can save their life."

Trust becomes a matter of life and death. Some may never have trusted anyone, others may have been betrayed by people they trusted. Many of our clients suffered some kind of childhood sexual abuse, and we need them to discuss, in detail, a horror they have certainly never resolved and may have kept buried for decades. Understanding the narratives they were enacting informed our own actions. It helped us understand their behavior, which might have been hard to understand had we not attempted to reflect on the narratives that might control them. Understanding their narratives helped us understand their actions and led to more successful interactions.

One mitigator told me about the mother of a client she wanted to have testify at her son's death penalty sentencing hearing. She wanted the mother to describe what her son's life was like growing up, hoping the jury would find mitigating evidence in hearing his life story. The mother had been abused by her second husband and was embarrassed about staying in the marriage. She did not want to testify. She was going by an all too common narrative in which people blame themselves for the abuse that happens to them. She was afraid that the jury would look down on her and wonder how she could stay in an abusive relationship. The mother herself did not understand her own actions. She knew she should have left, but couldn't. She did not question the narrative that kept her in the abusive relationship. I knew this aspect all too well; people will continue to enact a narrative even if it is detrimental to them.

This mother was also in deep denial about knowing that her son Leon had been molested and raped on an almost nightly basis from the time he was four until he was twelve, when he ran away. The mother felt helpless that she couldn't stop the abuse, and she lived in fear. If she began to bring it up, she was severely beaten, and her son got the same. She was afraid it might get worse if she tried to stop it, so she began to accept (or live in denial of) the abuse. If she tried to stop it, her husband might kill Leon. Reenacting that narrative kept her and her child stuck in a horrifying situation. To keep things from getting even worse, she accepted an unconscionable level of abuse. If Leon complained of being hungry, the husband made Leon eat rotting garbage. If the boy threw it up, he made him eat that too. The mother got the same unpredictable treatment and had a mentality of fear and silence that would never go away, even after the danger was long past. She had few interactions with her son after he ran away, so coming back now to testify at his death penalty trial seemed surreal. She had not seen her son in years and did not recognize him as an adult.

"I don't know him anymore," she said.

Leon had grown up in a silent rage and was so damaged that he conflated abuse with love. As a four-year-old, Leon had loved the person who also abused him when night came. Now Leon had become an abuser as well, and he had killed someone. He was facing the death penalty, and it was up to us to tell his whole story, to explain how Leon got to be this way, to make the jury understand how there were mitigating circumstances that might reduce his culpability enough to spare his life. To testify in open court, the mother would have to resist the control of lifelong narratives.

"Heck, she didn't even want to tell the jury about the horrible living conditions her son grew up in. She didn't want the jury to know they sometimes went without power when they couldn't pay the bills. She said that made her look like a bad mother. She was certainly never going to agree to speak about the abuse."

"So how would you get her to tell Leon's story?" I asked the mitigator.

"I had to get confrontational. It was risky after all I had done to gain her trust," the mitigator said. She essentially showed this mother how sticking to a narrative of silence led to a bleak outcome. "I laid it out for her: 'So you watched him get raped every night, and said nothing. Now you're going to watch him get killed, and say nothing?'"

She agreed to testify.

■ ■ ■

In preparing for change, consider all the narratives you are up against. Reflect on any dominant narratives and the forces that established their dominance. Become aware of the narratives others are going by as well as any narratives you are going by unconsciously. Work to deconstruct these narratives and replace them with new ones. Some narratives persist because you keep reenacting them with no more rationale than "that's the way things have always been done." In other instances, powerful legitimating forces will pressure you to continue to enact old narratives. This type of reflection will inform you of the difficultly you may have in creating and enacting new narratives. Just as the current paradigm resists the new paradigm, current narratives will be a source of resistance against the new narrative you are attempting to enact.

■ ■ ■

Uber was being ravaged by its own narratives as people there continued to enact them. Susan found a new team within Uber, but she continued to meet people who had experienced what she had. It was always the same story: his first offense, he is a high performer, the victim had to make a change, not Uber. It is incorrect to say that management never took action. They did, it was just the wrong action. They kept reenacting a narrative that was detrimental to Uber.

Given Uber's narratives, you will not be surprised to hear that employees were also pressured to undermine and backstab each other in pursuit of high performance. Employees at Uber must have believed they were benefiting from enacting these narratives, and it may have seemed so personally, but it left the organization in complete chaos. Projects were started and abandoned. Uber burned through money. Priorities seemed to change daily as teams formed and dissolved at an unrelenting pace. For many dissatisfied with the culture and its disarray, the only way to resist was to leave, so they did, in droves. Uber was bleeding talent. Guess who stayed? People who conformed to the narrative: backstabbers and jerks. If the enactment of these detrimental narratives continued, the existence of the company would soon be in doubt.

A talented engineer, Susan had lots of other job offers, and she finally took one. On the day she left Uber, of the 150 engineers in her area, only 3 percent were female. That number would continue to dwindle. It was not just the women who left. Anyone too smart to be pressured by the "bro culture" at Uber took his or her talent elsewhere. At the expense of keeping its narratives, Uber was sawing off its own limbs.

After she left, Susan shared her own narrative in a post titled "Reflecting on one very, very strange year at Uber." It went viral. As a result, the board of directors hired former U.S. Attorney General Eric Holder to conduct an investigation of the company culture at Uber.

■ ■ ■

In preparing for James Neely's trial, I worked on a narrative to counteract those we knew the jury would be going by. James was awarded a retrial on punishment only, so the jury would be instructed that he was guilty and that they were only there to determine a new punishment. I knew I had to contend with several narratives. I would have to deconstruct the preconceptions about how jury deliberations work and supply a new narrative for the jurors' deliberations. Even if I managed to do that, I had to counteract the misleading 10-2 rule in Texas that falsely led the jury to believe they all had to agree on a sentence.

I would spend many sleepless nights figuring out how to craft a new narrative that the jurors would accept. One they would enact over the powerful narratives they already held. One that might save James's life.

■ ■ ■

Meanwhile, back at Texas Tech, things were not going well for me. I was in my own trial of sorts, preparing to go up for tenure. My focus on fighting the death penalty for the past few years had put a dent in my research productivity. My publications came at a trickle. When you are a professor, gaps in research productivity raise a lot of questions about what you've been doing. I told myself I was doing a greater good for society, but the dominant narrative in the business school—one shared across academia— was publish or perish. I was about to perish.

A jury of my colleagues had begun a series of meetings to determine whether I would be awarded tenure. The last two tenure candidates in my department had been rejected, an unpromising trend. I already had a strike against me for being a qualitative researcher, and I appeared to be making horrible decisions on how I spent my time. I was devoting all my attention to fighting the death penalty, working alone on a single research project.

Researchers usually have several projects going, with multiple sets of colleagues, at various stages in the research process, building a steady pipeline of publications. It was smart. I was supposed to be writing papers, not saving killers. I had a good reputation in some academic circles, but those circles were small and way off the beaten path. Some colleagues had commented that my work on the death penalty had become a distraction.

"You should have spent more time publishing papers and less time in prisons," one colleague told me. His tenure vote would be no.

Most business schools brag about how their faculty's research brings the latest knowledge into the classroom. Our research enriches our teaching because we teach cutting-edge developments. I was warned not to talk about mine. The death penalty is such a controversial topic, they said. In the old days, the university was one of the few places where controversial topics got consideration. Now that kind of insight and reflection are discouraged.

"Consider your audience," I was admonished. I did. No one needs critical thought more than U.S. business school students. I was reminded several times that I should have done things the way things have always been done in academia, and that my prospects for tenure were uncertain.

Ironically, my convictions had given my life direction, and my work fighting the death penalty had become very meaningful and significant to me. Not many business school faculty members find their work to be meaningful, and only half of us report being satisfied in our jobs. I tried to tell myself that whatever happened regarding tenure I would be fine, but my fate kept me up nights with tightness in my chest.

Between my tenure fate and fighting the brutal death penalty system, when I did sleep, I had my first drunk dreams in years. I had seen many crime scene photos, and even sat in cells with the people responsible for the carnage, but my nightmares were about drinking, not murders—about booze, not blood. Drunk dreams are more common for people in early sobriety. You have vivid dreams that you have gotten drunk and ruined your life all over again, that everything you built in recovery has come crashing down. Drunk dreams can be a sign of stress, a dangerous one. These nightmares can be quite traumatic. You wake with anxiety and spend several minutes convincing yourself it didn't really happen—you did not blow your hard-earned recovery from addiction. It fills you with fear. That I began to have drunk dreams scared me. Was my sobriety in danger?

The work to change the death penalty sustained me somehow, and I couldn't stop, even as the costs mounted. If this was an unhealthy obsession, it would not be the first time I could not stop something that was hurting me. However, I was not sure that this was the case. The work required a lot of compassion, and by definition compassion involves suffering. The Latin root *passion* means "to suffer," and the prefix *co* means "with." When you help those who are suffering, you suffer alongside them. Compassion is also good for the world—and you. Gandhi said, "If you want others to be happy, practice compassion. If you want to be happy, practice compassion."

When change is hard and you are leading that change, you might expect some pain and suffering. It is not news to recognize that change can be difficult, consuming, and exhausting.

But it is also rewarding.

6
Enacting New Narratives

"**L**et's get started again then," said Judge Hatch. The judge had spent half the morning monotonously rejecting our defense motions, one after another, and we still had a lot to go. The judge had ruled only once in our favor, and it was on a technicality.

We were in court for a pretrial hearing on James Neely's case, arguing motions about what would happen during trial. We filed a motion for individual voir dire during jury selection, in which potential jurors take the stand one at a time and are questioned about their views, instead of in a group. Individual voir dire is common practice in capital trials, but you still have to file a motion to make it official. In fact, the DA had filed the same motion.

"Granted!" Judge Hatch snickered. "Glad I could finally give ya' one." Even though this tickled him, he held the defense team in disdain.

We had also filed a motion to take turns with the prosecution when questioning jurors. The prosecution always goes first, and then the juror is passed to the defense. This norm is a spillover from trial, where the prosecution presents a case and then the defense responds. In jury selection in death penalty cases, the DA spends a lot of time coaching jurors on how to answer questions the defense may ask. Their goal is to make sure people in favor of the death penalty know how to answer questions to remain eligible for jury duty. If the DA likes the potential juror, the DA literally tells the juror what to say to make sure he or she is not disqualified from the jury. In this coaching, the DA comes very close to telling jurors to lie so they are not dismissed. We filed a motion to at least take turns going first during jury selection so we would get straight answers at least half of the time.

"Denied!" The judge shouted over his own chuckling and coughing. By this time, he was well back into the swing of saying no, stacking the deck against us. Toby, the lead defense attorney, kept going down our long list of motions.

"The next, Your Honor," Toby said, "is a motion to find the 10-2 rule unconstitutional."

Judge Hatch gave a disinterested wave for Toby to continue.

"The jury receives improper information that leads them to believe they must have at least ten jurors to vote for a life sentence. Thus the jury deliberates under false instructions. Furthermore, no one is allowed to tell the jury the true effect of a non-unanimous decision, which is an automatic life without parole." Toby contends it is "misinformation for jurors" and leads to "jury confusion" about mistrials or hung juries, which the court is not allowed to clarify. "Even if jurors specifically ask, I cannot give them the correct information, and neither can you." Toby argues that the 10-2 rule violates the Eighth Amendment, "which says one juror is entitled to return a life sentence. But if they deliberated under the false information that they need nine other jurors to join them, they capitulate and give death." Toby adds that it is "coercive" and cites Supreme Court law that says the court is bound to provide the jury with enough information to allow for "informed deliberation." He lists a string of additional violations under the Fifth, Sixth, Eighth, and Four-teenth Amendments to "the Constitution of the United States."

"Denied," Judge Hatch sighed and banged the gavel. "How many more of these have we got, anyways?" It was almost lunchtime.

"Quite a few," said Toby.

"They aren't just more constitutional ones, are they?"

"I'm afraid so, Your Honor." Toby wasn't afraid at all.

We would argue over eighty motions in pretrial hearings. Some were small, such as a motion for James to be able to wear a suit instead of the jail issued orange jumpsuit during trial, because seeing James in prison garb and chains would definitely bias jury perceptions about whether or not James was a future danger to society and needed to be killed. There were also dozens of motions to find the death penalty itself unconstitutional, on all kinds of grounds.

We expected to be denied on all of them, but we still filed and argued them. Toby and Graham, the defense attorneys, argued each motion meticulously. Judge Hatch had stated explicitly, perhaps taken off guard by how dedicated Toby and Graham seemed to be, that he was not going to be declaring anything unconstitutional. He was flummoxed by their persistence.

We were not really arguing the motions for this judge anyway. We were enacting our new narrative of *perfect the record*. Toby and Graham were looking way ahead, arguing to the Supreme Court, which might eventually review this death penalty case. Each motion to find the death penalty unconstitutional was a lifeline for James Neely. Toby and Graham were also leaving breadcrumbs so any Supreme Court decision, even on other cases with the same issues, might find its way back to James.

The main purpose of this narrative, expecting to be overruled in this court, was to get the motions into the official court record for eventual appeals. We expected nothing from Hatch. He said many times that finding any part of the death penalty unconstitutional "was above my pay grade." To be fair, judges usually stick to precedent. The result is that the system becomes more and more institutionalized. From a case law perspective, the death penalty has gotten stronger and stronger. In Texas, the Court of Criminal Appeals has become a virtual upholding court, not an appellate court.

Given the insurmountable odds of a favorable ruling on any motion to find the death penalty unconstitutional, many trial lawyers do not even bother to file the motions. This common practice among death penalty defense attorneys cuts off a future lifeline for their clients. Perfecting the record was very much a cultural change in the practice of death penalty defense in Texas. My team had garnered legitimacy and influence by providing much of the training to death penalty qualified attorneys around Texas, and the practice was becoming more and more common, with more attorneys enacting this narrative.

Judge Hatch was not even paying attention to the arguments. But again, who cares? We were talking to the Supreme Court through the record we were creating. So Toby remained diligent, speaking clearly and slowly enough so that the court stenographer could hear things exactly as he phrased them. One day— some day many years from now—when this trial is well into the appellate process, the ruling on that very motion denied today may be the one the Supreme Court overturns. James Neely may be awarded yet another trial, perhaps a fair one.

The Supreme Court ruling that helps James may not even be from his own trial. Perhaps the Supreme Court will review another death penalty case in Texas and find the 10-2 rule to be unconstitutional. If you do not file a motion in your own case, any Supreme Court rulings on other cases do not apply to your case. The Supreme Court will grant relief to other cases that raised the exact same issue. "You can lose the trial and still win your case," I once told an attorney during a training session. "What you do in trial could win the case in twenty years."

So we are going through the motions, literally, knowing that we are perfecting the official court record. It is a snowball's chance in hell, but it's a chance—that is, if we file and if the courts rule on the issue and if James is still alive.

■ ■ ■

You gained an understanding of just what we are up against in challenging powerful narratives in chapter 5. I want to turn your attention now to the right side of our model: enacting change. Transformational change involves a vision of a better future, and it calls for others to internalize that vision to provide a shared sense of purpose. Creating and enacting a narrative achieves all of these elements of transformational change.

Creating a new narrative is not simple, and you will face many constraints. The most important constraint in creating a new narrative is that it *must* be done with material already in our cognitive frameworks. We have to use materials on hand, so to speak, from our current stocks of knowledge. Change nearly always consists of refashioning existing ideas—constructing something new with old materials. We must piece together what we already know in new and different ways. The good news is that we have all the material we need. And fear not, you can build a beautiful palace with old materials.

To illustrate this reconstruction with materials on hand, I often ask my students this question: "How would you describe windsurfing to someone who had never seen it?"

"You could tell them it is like surfing, but with a sail from a sailboat attached to a surfboard," one person says.

"Yes," I agree, "but what would they have to know to understand that description?"

"They would have to know what surfing and sailing are," someone says.

"Exactly. They would have to have those concepts in their heads already, or our description would make no sense to them. That is a big challenge in both learning and change. The only way to explain a new concept to someone, other than firsthand experience, is to recombine concepts they already know to create brand new concepts."

In the death penalty context, I created a new narrative to teach jurors what deliberations are actually like. My intention was to counteract the 10-2 rule without breaking the law that states you cannot inform a jury of the true result (a life sentence) of their inability to agree on a sentence. I used concepts I was confident the jurors already had in their heads to instill a new narrative and a new way of thinking. This narrative was used during questioning of potential jurors to see if the defense wanted them on the jury. This is one of the many narratives we created in fighting the death penalty.

Traditionally, the defense approach to jury selection was to try to find out what made a potential juror tick, and then to use armchair psychology to pick jurors the defense thought would vote for life. It was not uncommon, for example, for lawyers to ask what kind of bumper stickers jurors had on their cars, or even to send snoops to find this out. The idea of using voir dire to educate a juror was somewhat innovative, and our team implemented this narrative vigorously during jury selection.

This approach produced a dramatic shift in the defense team's goal for voir dire. Instead of using this time *to find out* what's in a juror's head, we used this time *to put stuff in* a juror's head—to educate the juror. "If you want to know what's in a juror's head," I said during death penalty certification seminars, "then put it in there. It's the only way to be certain. You need to change minds, not read them." Instead of trying to interpret vague clues, defense attorneys can educate the jurors and introduce new concepts to them during voir dire. This was an attractive notion for defense attorneys because the average person's concept of sentencing deliberations was incorrect. Moreover, those misconceptions strongly favor the prosecution and lead to death sentences.

Most everyone already has an idea—a false narrative—of what deliberations are like. The main misimpression jurors hold is that they must all come to agreement on a sentence or there will be a mistrial. But, as you now know, jurors are really only deciding whether to up the sentence to death. If they cannot agree, the sentence remains life without parole. They get these ideas from social norms about majority rules or even movies and TV crime shows or legal dramas. Some of these narratives do resemble trial deliberations on guilt or innocence, but deliberations during a sentencing hearing in a death penalty case is a unique situation.

I created a new narrative by rearranging concepts in jurors' heads, but I also had to get jurors to resist going by the narratives they had learned from society. This can be a daunting part of any change process. In death penalty seminars, I addressed the attorneys as if they were in a mock trial, role playing with them as potential jurors.

"Hello ladies and gentlemen. If the defendant is found guilty, there will be a sentencing hearing, the second phase of a capital trial. You will be asked to deliberate on whether the defendant is sentenced to life without parole, or death. [pause] Have any of you ever participated in a death penalty trial? [pause] Okay, so none of you have ever done this, but do you have an idea of what deliberations are like?"

It is highly unlikely people will have served on jury, and even less likely that they have served on a death penalty case. What a startling juxtaposition—no one has ever done this, but they all have ideas about how it happens. These are the narratives we want them to avoid enacting. It will kill our client. We want to construct a new narrative for them and encourage them to go by that one instead. But first we have to discourage them from mindlessly applying what they think they know.

"Whatever you think jury deliberations are like," I say, "I can promise you that deliberations are not like that. [pause] Since none of you have ever been on a capital jury, let's compare it to some things I bet you have all done. Have you ever been to the movies with a group of people?"

The attorneys in the training session are being a good audience. They nod along.

"So what happens? Let's say you all meet at the movie theater. You all stare at the marquee to see what's playing and make a collective decision on what to see, right? Let's say there are only two movies playing. What happens? You talk about it and decide which of the two movies you will all go see." There are nods; everyone has been to the movies with friends and decided which movie to see this way. Using two movies in this narrative, it is obvious that I am setting them up for a life or death decision.

"Deliberations are NOT like that," I tell them, hoping they will begin to question their existing narratives. "Now, how many of you have been to dinner with a big group of people?" Everyone nods. "Deliberations are like that," I say. "So what happens there? You all go to dinner, and you sit around the table, and you look at a menu, and *you each* decide what *you* want to order. And the *server* comes in and takes your order." I am choosing my words very carefully, and you will see why soon. "They simply take your order, right? The server does not ask, 'How could you order fish?' And if the person next to you orders steak, but you want fish, is that a problem?" It is rhetorical now.

"No, of course not! You each put in *your own order*. Unlike choosing a movie, at a group dinner you each get to pick whatever you want, and it is totally independent of what anyone else picks. You don't have to agree. The server doesn't say, 'You all have to order the same thing,' does she? No. Never. Everyone makes an individual decision. Everyone gets what they want. Unlike picking which movie to see, you do not all have to agree on what to order."

The analogy is obvious by now, and I hope this narrative is easy for them to remember. "Other people may ask you about your order, or what you think you'll have, but they don't get to tell you what to order. You put in *your own order*." I hope they feel empowered now. "And the *server* just takes it. That's all the server does, simply takes your order. That's what sentencing deliberations are like, and the judge is like your server."

I use this analogy because I want to put the jurors in charge. They actually are in charge—they just don't realize it. This narrative has two aims. One is to let them know that they do not all have to agree, and the other is to empower them to stick to their decision.

To stick to their resolve, these jurors will have to resist some powerful cultural norms. For the entire trial, the judge has told the jurors when to show up, when they can eat or sit, and even when they can go to the bathroom. The judge sits up higher than everyone else in the courtroom, elevated both physically and socially. Nothing starts until the judge arrives (last), and nothing stops until the judge says so. Everyone stands when the judge enters or leaves the room. All of that symbolism creates an image of an all-powerful ruler rather than a humble servant of the court.

"Just like the server," I continue with my mock jurors, "the judge will never, ever, ask you to explain your order. He can't." I let that sink in. The idea that the judge cannot do things will be something that jurors have not considered. "The Supreme Court has ordered him not to." This positions the judge more correctly in their eyes. Judges have to follow orders too, not just give them. I next turn to how they might regard their fellow jurors. "And none of the other people at the table have a right to compel you to order anything you don't want, do they? The judge might ask you to try and keep deliberating, but if you have made up your mind on your order, no one can ask you to change it, and you do not have to continue deliberating or thinking about it. You can say you have thought about it and that you are done deliberating. Most important, you *do not* all have to agree. Deliberations are like going to dinner with a group of people, *not* like going to a movie with a group of people. You are done deliberating when *you* say so, no one else." I am dismissing the narrative they already have and encouraging them to adopt my new narrative, one constructed from materials and situations with which they are already familiar.

I close with a question asking for their commitment. "Do you all think you can remember that when deliberations start? It may be several weeks from now before deliberations start, but I want you to remember this. If you reach a sentencing hearing and deliberate on a sentence, it is not like going to the movies where you all have to agree. It is like going to dinner with a group of people. You get to put in your own individual order. Everyone does. You don't bully anyone into ordering your choice, and conversely, no one should bully you into ordering something you don't want. You can all talk about your orders, and people can ask you to think about all your options, to deliberate, but in the end, *your order* is *your individual decision*. And you don't have to explain yourself to anyone. I promise you, the judge won't even ask. He is not allowed to ask. You are in charge, and you don't have to explain your order—to anyone. Do you think you will be able to remember that?"

I am so explicit, adamant, and repetitive when telling my narrative because the pressures to conform are nearly insurmountable. Recall from the Capital Jury Project that 99 percent of the time juries are not unanimous in voting for death during deliberations.[1] But almost every time they eventually delivered a death sentence. I hope this narrative provides enough empowerment for a juror to survive the extreme pressures of being a holdout.

Out of the entire trial process, jury selection is the best place to plant this narrative. Closing arguments at the sentencing hearing, which occurs right before juries begin deliberations, provides a final opportunity for the defense to remind jurors of this narrative and encourage them to go by it. I think this narrative greatly improves the chance of saving a life.

As you can see, the lesson for leading change addresses two important issues. We must construct a new narrative—the new way of doing things—and we must encourage people to enact that narrative rather than continuing the old way of doing things. My experience fighting the death penalty has heightened my awareness of this challenge.

Many of the changes made in the death penalty setting involved the professional culture of defense attorneys. We had to change the way attorneys thought. The first change was to the culture of not wanting to cross the judge or suffer a variety of sanctions. As previously explained, the judge is often in charge of assigning defense attorneys on court-appointed cases. If the defense attorneys irritate the judge, they are unlikely to get work in the future. Going against the judge, even to help a client, could be a threat to their livelihood. As part of our new narrative, we became more client-focused and eschewed pandering to judges. We would file funding motions and almost dare the judge to say no, suggesting that the Supreme Court would overturn the trial if they did. This gained us no friends on the bench, but a lot of respect from judges.

■ ■ ■

Change action loops describe the main aim of our narrative change process. By enacting a new narrative, not only do we change the way things are done, we position the narrative in our cognitive framework. It has a chance to take.[2] For example, the new narrative may become part of the organizational culture and itself one day be taken for granted as the way we do things around here.

Change action loops occur when we choose a new narrative to guide our actions, behaviors, and interpretations (see figure 6.1). When we use a new narrative of the way we see things, we bring

Figure 6.1 Change action loops

Source: Figure by the author

it into being in the real world and give it a chance to become institutionalized in our cognitive framework. If the new narrative is more and more widely shared through ongoing enactment, it becomes part of our culture—be it organizational or societal.[3]

Narratives are socially constructed; we make them. Anthropologists point out that our collective ways of taking action emerge from group problem solving.[4] When something works, it becomes a narrative for how a particular situation is approached, and over time we develop a routine response whenever that problem arises. This implies some happenstance and guesswork out of an emergent process of trial and error. Larger-scale social or cultural change follows the same narrative change process I have described. It may take longer, but the same processes are at work.

■ ■ ■

During Seth Rose's trial, we used the narrative about deliberations being like going to dinner rather than going to the movies to combat the 10-2 rule. I worked with the defense team on that case. The attorneys focused on deconstructing the narratives we knew jurors had, namely, that there would be a mistrial. They told jurors that it was not true, and that a jury split on sentencing still resulted in a "successful trial" instead of a mistrial, going right up to, but not over, the line of informing them what *would* happen as a result of an inability to agree, which was a life sentence by default.

Robin Conley-Riner, an anthropologist from UCLA doing her dissertation on capital juries, interviewed several jurors who sat on the jury in the Seth Rose trial. "They were the only jurors I ever talked to who knew what they were actually voting on," she told me.[5] It was evident that our narrative had indeed informed them about how deliberations actually worked. This was great news for the prospects of our new narrative.

■ ■ ■

After the pretrial hearing in James Neely's case, I went with Larry Calvert, one of our mitigators, to measure James for a suit he would wear during trial. At the jail, we sat with James in a visitation cell. I was taking field notes and jotted down the measurements while Larry wrapped the measuring tape around James's shoulders, then his waist.

James did not like being touched. He had already asked us to spread the word to everyone on the team that he liked them all very much, but he preferred fist bumps to handshakes. James had spent almost twenty years alone in a 10×6 foot cell. The only human contact he had was a guard's gloved hand on his back as he was moved about death row, and touching now made him uncomfortable.

■ ■ ■

Near the end of my drinking, I felt like I was suspended over a bottomless crevasse, holding the ends of a rope in each hand. I was being torn in half. I clung to each rope for dear life, the abyss beneath me. The ropes were significant. On one hand, I wanted everything to be okay. I wanted to stop hurting. I wanted the anger writhing in me to dissipate. On the other hand, I wanted to keep drinking. I could not imagine my life without alcohol.

No matter how hard I tried, pulled, and yanked, I could not get the ends of those two ropes to come together. It was never going to happen. I couldn't keep drinking and be okay. I could not hang on much longer.

I had to let go.

■ ■ ■

Back on campus, department deliberations about my tenure were well underway. Things were not looking good, and I was mentally preparing myself for the news that a lot of academics got. I still had no idea what I would do if I didn't get tenure. Most faculty moved on to smaller schools with higher teaching loads. Maybe that would not be too bad.

Michael kept prodding me to go to law school. "It would be easy for you," he assured me. "Why not just go ahead and become a defense attorney?"

"And go broke?" I joked. I also told him I thought I was better built to fight the death penalty the way I had been. Regardless of the costs of the choices I had made, I was willing to accept them. I had resigned myself to my fate. If my convictions cost me tenure, I would accept that as a small price to pay for having found something so deeply meaningful. Tenure is pretty rare, but not as rare as a fulfilling life.

7

Narrative Selection Versus Narrative Construction

Now that we understand how narratives shape our behavior and actions, let's look at the entire process. In this chapter, the construction and enactment of new narratives is discussed in more detail. Recall what we are trying to achieve: If we all go by narratives naturally, can we intentionally create a new narrative and go by it?

Enacting a new narrative changes the way we see things so we can change the way we act. In addition to understanding the entire selection versus creation process, we need to understand the four modes of narrative enactment: unconscious enactment, conscious enactment, reconstruction (autopilot), and intentional reconstruction. By looking at whether narrative enactment happens by selection or construction, and whether we are conscious, deliberate, and purposeful, or unconsciously enacting an existing narrative, we can determine which narrative mode is operating during the action.

Figure 7.1 illustrates the narrative enactment process. It begins when a salient event initiates a sense-making process. The salient event may be something we observe or it may be an interaction we have with someone else. We may encounter a situation that calls for a decision, even a common one, such as returning an

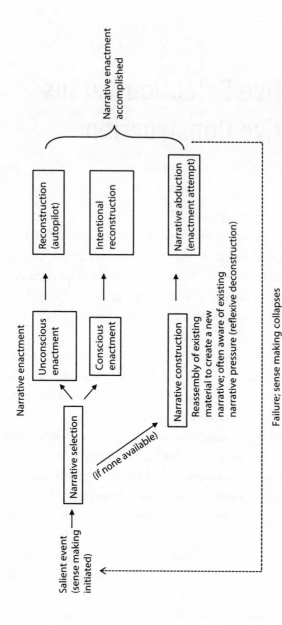

Figure 7.1 An illustration of the narrative enactment process

Source: Figure by the author

item to a store. The first thing we do in any situation is search our mind for a narrative to guide us through the situation. We have narratives for almost all of the situations we encounter. Even if the event is a first for us, such as a first date, or something uncomfortable, such as a relationship breakup, we already have a narrative to enact to help us navigate this interaction because we have seen this narrative in movies or heard stories about it from friends.

We have a narrative we often apply unconsciously on a first date. Perhaps this event entails dinner and a movie, and it has become so ingrained that we take them to be synonymous.

"Do you want to go out?"

"Sure, where should we eat? What's playing at the theater?"

Unconscious enactment of a narrative results in reconstruction of the way things have always been done. Unconscious enactment stabilizes rather than changes. Reconstructing an existing narrative engrains or institutionalizes it even more. We are not reflexive about the narrative we are going by; our actions are on autopilot.

At other times, we are more conscious of the narrative we are going by in making sense of a situation. We purposefully decide to go by a narrative. Enacting it helps us accomplish some interaction. If we are successful, the narrative becomes more institutionalized. If we believe it worked well for us, we are likely to use it the next time we are in a similar situation.

A fairly new narrative has become common in the dating world: ghosting. You break up with someone by abruptly disappearing and blocking all methods of contact. You become a ghost. Instead of having a conversation about ending the relationship, the unfortunately popular ghosting narrative guides us to simply and suddenly quit communicating with our partner. You no longer send or respond to texts or emails. You delete or block the person from social media contact. A key part of this narrative is that ceasing contact is unannounced. Breaking off contact after breaking up may be fine, even recommended, but to do it unannounced, as with ghosting, is a way to avoid confrontation. The old narrative for a breakup, if I may show my age, called for having an uncomfortable conversation in which one of the partners announces his or her intention to end the relationship. This may be followed by an announced intention, or even an agreement, to stop all communications. In the ghosting narrative, the first step is skipped, leaving one partner wondering what happened and why. It is human nature to want to know why. Dating etiquette still calls for at least a breakup text and recognition of receipt, but students tell me that ghosting has become so widespread that it is a highly recognizable narrative. It is a social norm that is no longer confusing.

"It has become obvious when someone ghosts you now," one student told me when I brought it up as a class topic. "You know they're blowing you off. If they don't want to tell you it's over, that's fine, it just reflects on their character."

"No one is bewildered?" I ask.

"Not anymore," someone says. It seems the ghosting narrative has become popular enough that people are now beginning to respond to it as a socially acceptable breakup method. "They should have the courtesy to send a text, at least, but if they don't, it's not hard to figure out that it's over and they're ghosting you."

"I prefer to be ghosted," someone interjects.

"Now that's surprising," I say. "Why?"

"I went through a traditional breakup where my girlfriend of two years told me she met someone else," he said. "I wish she would have just ghosted me." As I type this, it strikes me that he used the term *traditional breakup*. That illustrates how much the dating world has changed!

"Yeah, but at least you know what happened," another student says.

"I would have rather had no explanation than that one," he retorted.

A few others agreed that being ghosted, although still categorized as impolite, allowed you to spare some of your own feelings, and in the absence of an explanation, you could invent a palatable reason.

"When I was in college," I said, "I would have thought someone I cared about was dead or missing! The uncertainty, the wondering what could have happened, would have been horrible. Shocking."

"Yeah," they shrug. "No one thinks like that anymore."

A quick hand survey ascertains that nobody is confused by ghosting anymore. Plus, the students assure me, friends of friends are so interconnected on social media that it is easy to confirm that the person who disappeared from your life is perfectly fine. "Your friends tell you they see them posting pictures of themselves out at parties or on vacation. It's easy to tell they have just moved on."

Ghosting still feels cruel to me, but this new narrative makes sense of an interaction and seems to be accepted as mainstream by those who grew up with smartphones and social media. It has become more and more institutionalized.

Instead of selecting a narrative, we can create one via narrative construction. Constructing and enacting new narratives has been the main focus of this book. However, I still want to point out that being aware of how the existing narratives we select without thought is a major hurdle in accomplishing change. Breaking free from the way things have always been done is the biggest challenge in establishing a new way of doing things.

Narrative construction must be done with materials on hand. We take concepts already in our minds and reassemble them in new ways to construct new narratives. Deconstructing old narratives can free up material for creating new ones. Deconstruction and construction are two components of one change process. Deconstruction means we critically question, as opposed to take for granted, the way things are done. In doing so, we challenge a narrative's control over the way we see and do things—this is the heart of critical thinking. This requires that we are reflexive about all the narratives we go by. We become hyperconscious of why we are doing things the way we do, and cease to accept "because that's the way it's always been done" as a legitimate rationale.

Narrative construction and enactment is an *abductive* process.[1] Abduction may be a new term for you. It attends to the unknown and yet to be—events that fit no known pattern. It stands in contrast to two better known logic processes: deduction and induction. *Deduction* draws logical conclusions based on the known, and *induction* categorizes specific instances into known categories. Just as narrative construction is much rarer than narrative selection, abduction is much less discussed, and less common, than deduction or induction.

Deductive thinking begins with general premises and leads to a logical conclusion. When I was a kid, I preferred that my parents arrive at some facts via deduction rather than through a direct confession from me. I might lay out the first premise for her: "Mom, everyone in class got in trouble today." Then I add another to help her connect the dots on her own: "And, as you know, I would never skip class." She could deduce the logical conclusion from these two premises.

Induction begins with a specific case and draws on a general category to make sense of an observation or situation. This categorization is a form of pattern recognition. We make sense of a situation, categorize it, and then select an appropriate narrative to apply. It moves from a particular situation to a general label. All narrative selection, whether conscious or unconscious, involves inductive thinking. Every time you have an interaction or situation, you search your mind for a similar category of patterns and categorize your current interaction as falling into that general situation. You then select a narrative to guide you through that situation, and this narrative helps you make decisions, navigate the situation, or accomplish the interaction. You get a stuffy nose and a sore throat and induce that you must have a cold by categorizing your symptoms. You initiate your cold narrative, part of which might direct you to make chicken soup. If a dress you bought online does not fit you correctly, you might declare it a return situation and enact the narrative that fits that pattern, one that has you shipping it back to the company and expecting to see your account credited in a few days.

Abduction is a third type of logic that results in a whole new ballgame. Scratch that—a whole new game altogether! It requires creation of a new category driven by a novel situation. Instead of pattern recognition, it is pattern creation. Abductive thinking is the only way to produce new knowledge. This construction uses existing materials, but the concepts are put together in a whole new way. In narrating change, abduction results in an entirely new way of doing things that does not fit into any existing categories.

Facing new and unique situations might drive us to create entirely new concepts and categories. Abduction is akin to a paradigm shift, in which a new category results in recategorizing much of what we thought we knew, changing the way we think about a large area of our knowledge. For example, think of the work of paleontologists. When they find a fossil, they attempt to categorize it into existing categories. But sometimes the fossil doesn't fit into any existing category. An object or experience that cannot be categorized, or labeled, is an anomaly. We struggle to make sense of anomalies and try to place them or match them to a pattern.

This was exactly the case in the early 1860s with the discovery of the *Archaeopteryx*, a fossil that had feathers like a bird but also had teeth! Further inspection revealed a unique type of clawed foot and bones in the tail—features unlike anything in the bird category. This find caused scientists to produce an entirely new category of animal that linked birds and dinosaurs much closer than previously thought. This made it necessary to revise and reconstruct large parts of the existing biological taxonomy. The new category caused scientists to question much of what they thought they already knew and to recategorize many existing species according to the entirely new taxonomic rankings. Everything changed.

One of my favorite examples of abductive thinking that changes the way things have always been done comes from a true story about firefighters.[2] A group of firefighters were fighting a fire on the northern Plains. One team found themselves separated and trapped in a gulch as the fire raced toward them. Some of the firefighters attempted to race up the sides of the steep brush-filled ravine, and others attempted to outrun the fast approaching fire. One firefighter stayed right where he was and used his equipment to light a fire right under his feet. That fire, too, began to rapidly spread outward from the center point, burning all the grass and brush and leaving an ever-widening circle of scorched earth. Inside the circle, there was nothing left to burn. The firefighter stood right in the middle of the scorched area as roaring fire hurdled toward him in the gulch. The fire split when it came to the preburned area and went wide around him, rejoining on the other side of the circle area and continuing down the gulch. He was the only survivor in his unit.

This abductive thinking created an entirely new response and reorganized survival methods for firefighters. The firefighter created the narrative with existing knowledge that had never been put together and used in this way. This new narrative about burning an approaching fire's fuel to remove fuel sources in its path is now widespread and institutionalized. This new narrative is part of every firefighter's cognitive framework and is available should they induce that they are in a similar situation.

Because narrative abduction is an entirely new way of doing things, there is no way to predict if it will work. You just have to try it. Because it is entirely new, we have no reason to believe it will or won't work. Literally, no reasoning is available yet because it is so novel. As figure 7.1 shows, narrative abduction is the attempted enactment of a new narrative.

Abductive processing has huge implications for change. There is no way to use existing knowledge to make a case for new knowledge. We cannot rely on the way things have always been done to convince people that the new way will work. We just have to take a leap of faith and see what happens. It is nice, because the proof is in the "putting," not in the convincing. We enact the new narrative and see if it works. If it is successful, we keep the new narrative as part of our cognitive framework and use it more and more often. If it keeps working, we keep enacting it, and it becomes more and more solidified or institutionalized. If it fails, we begin the process over again, selecting another narrative or creating one.

To close this discussion on narrative enactment, recognize that enacting a new way of doing things, once institutionalized, eventually becomes the old way of doing things. That's right, from the start we know that our new way of doing things may one day become the way things have always been done. And that narrative may need to be changed in the future. Figure 7.1 shows the circular process for creating new narratives.

▪ ▪ ▪

Uber will not survive without constructing and enacting a new narrative. Arianna Huffington, the only woman on the board of directors, vowed that a culture encouraging people to be "brilliant jerks" could not continue. As part of the narrative construction process, Uber will have to deconstruct the current narratives and create new narratives that promote the kind of culture to which they aspire.

Eric Holder began deconstruction of Uber's current narratives by exposing them. Uber's narratives had encouraged bad behavior to permeate the company. Holder's report unveiled hundreds of harassment claims. A party culture and a bro code fostered inappropriate behavior, and other narratives pressured employees to undercut each other, exemplified by popular sayings at Uber like "always be hustlin'." A narrative called "let builders build" signaled that high performers had free rein to behave however they wanted. Other narratives, such as "toe-stepping," encouraged confrontation. There was zero trust inside of Uber.

When it was all laid out on the table, Uber held a company-wide meeting to discuss the issues. It did not go well. Employees said management had no credibility. Seventy percent of employees said the meeting did nothing to change their perception about the culture at Uber, and more than 30 percent said they planned to leave the company. Externally, protesters marched to highlight the sexual harassment and mistreatment inside Uber.

Uber lost $4.5 billion in 2017. Travis Kalanick agreed to resign, but he left behind a toxic workplace that badly needed change.

■ ■ ■

Before we can bring a narrative to fruition through our actions, before we can choose to go by our new story, we must construct it. This can involve delicate craftsmanship with limited materials. New narratives are built with existing materials that already reside in our culturally shared, cognitive framework. Just as new ideas come from recombining old ideas, new narratives come from refashioning existing narratives. We have no choice but to use materials on hand, and taking them apart and putting them together in new ways can be difficult work.

Most change is incremental, and large-scale, transformational change is especially challenging. Seeing new ways to assemble old material requires a tremendous amount of creativity. In everyday life, even the newest ideas tend to closely resemble existing versions, as you will see in this classroom experiment.

I bang on a table in front of a classroom of fifty students. "What else could we make with this?" I ask. Students stare at the table and then at me. "You know, if we took this table apart and started all over with the parts. Everything here. What else could we build with these same materials?"

"A bench?" someone meekly suggests after a painfully long silence.

"Some chairs?" another student says.

This happens every time. Even as I beg them to be creative, their suggestions remain stuck in the furniture family. They are only able to see the materials in ways they have already been used.

"How about *another* table?" I ask sarcastically, but I can see half of them were actually about to suggest just that. "Come on gang, think."

"How about a bookcase?" someone says.

"Bravo!" I say. "That's much better. You can see we're moving a bit further away from the original use, but it's difficult to see old things used in new ways, right? Once we see these materials used for a table, it is hard to see the material as being useful for anything else."

A tremendous but often overlooked part of the change process is conceptualizing the new way of doing things in the first place. Creativity is a big piece of the puzzle to brush under the rug, yet it is just a special instance of change. The bulk of our advice surrounds implementation, getting people to accept a new way of doing things.

Science is guilty of this same focus on hypothesis testing and seemingly hasn't a care in the world about how hypotheses are created. We have libraries full of directions on hypothesis testing. But hypothesis creation requires abductive thinking, and the bolder the hypothesis the greater the advancement we stand to make. Even so, we have largely ignored the hypothesis creation step in science, just as change advice is heavy on implementation and light on idea creation.

In more than ten years in the classroom, no one has yet answered "a surfboard!" when I ask what else we could make from the materials used to make a table. The skills to build it are not that rare, and the construction work, the implementation, is pretty straightforward. Building is not the problem—creative design ideas are what we lack.

But we should not be too hard on ourselves. Given the chance to build anything we like, it is not a huge surprise to find ourselves remaking things in familiar ways. We keep reconstructing the same narratives rather than make new ones. This is not irrational; most of our narratives guide us reliably through recurring situations. We need that stability. But if we want a new way of doing and being, we need new narratives to enact.

To offer some practical advice for constructing new narratives, I am going to borrow inspiration from good storytelling. The process I facilitated with the death penalty defense team formalized and made explicit the naturally occurring social construction processes. In the narrative construction workshop, I called attention to these processes and gave the team time to reflect on them at a conscious and explicit level, which encouraged creativity. My aim was to create our story deliberately and consciously, to collectively agree to "make a narrative" and try to "go by" that narrative as a primary means of organizing. The steps we took in constructing the death penalty defense narrative can be applied to any organizational setting.

1. **Generate a list of characters.** Begin with a brainstorming session, and list all the characters who will play a role in your narrative. This includes every stakeholder you interact with in doing your work. The list may be several pages. For my team, it included our team members, DAs, judges, our client, jail snitches, various experts, family members, court administrators, gang affiliates, etc.

Whatever your setting, it is a good idea to take a very broad view of organizational stakeholders. Include your organizational members, but also customers, suppliers, and the community, but not some vague notion of the community. I encourage you to think of actual interactions that occur in your setting. Instead of community, think of characters in action. Who do you really mean when you say "community"? Do you mean people from the local high school? Put it on the list. To flesh out the list, reflect on a few questions about your daily interactions. Who do you communicate with via text message or emails? Who do you interact with in the course of your work? The length of the list might surprise you.

2. **Start your narrative in the middle.** Starting in the middle is tried and true writing advice. Start with an event, which will also kick off interpretation, sense making, and creative insights for the people involved in the narrative construction process. Do not begin with the company background or history. Leave the date you were founded to the company historian.

Begin your narrative with an action. It will orient you to enactment, and it is much more powerful. A customer calls with a complaint. A customer puts in an order. My team's narrative began with a murder. Your narrative might begin in the middle of your main practice, such as during an appointment, or if you work for an airline, perhaps in midflight—even a customer using your product could be a good place to start.

Think of what starting with an action does compared to describing your company's background. Here is an example of what not to do: "Back in 1989, Judy and Ted got together and started talking about how no one was really servicing at-home medical equipment." Boring. Story rigor mortis sets in before the narrative ever has a chance to move! Instead, start with a patient in a hospital wanting to be home who is held back only by lack of a basic piece of medical equipment that might easily be used at home and monitored remotely. That scene brings to life your reason for creating a medical equipment company.

3. **Categorize narrative actions.** As we constructed our death penalty defense narrative, we simultaneously categorized the actions in our narrative. We color-coded things that must occur (by legal or some other mandate), things that are likely

to occur (things the DA or other stakeholders typically do), and things we would like to occur (actions we alone initiate). Categorizing common actions in our narrative helped make sense of simultaneous actions that would occur as we enacted our plot line. It helped us retain and manage the complexity of the process. The narrative resembled a realistic current state of affairs, with concrete steps leading to future strategic hopes and dreams. The narrative was only loosely sequential because many actions can occur simultaneously. Organizing in this way helped lay out, in action, how we would get from here to there without brushing any details under the rug (as bullet points and many mainstream strategies or goals do). Our narrative not only recognized mutual interactions, showing how our actions were influenced by people outside of our team, but it also recognized that we might be able to influence others via our actions. This allowed us to be very proactive.

4. **Include your goals as well as other plausible outcomes.** Unlike a simple goal, a narrative entails both a goal and the detailed actions that help attain it. Presenting a goal to people can certainly motivate them, but letting them participate in constructing the narrative—their role and the actions that lead to achieving the goal—is much more powerful and useful. Narratives build in "actionability" but also maintain flexibility and an ability to improvise that strategies do not encompass. We included other plausible outcomes because we needed to be ready to change our path if we were headed toward an unwanted or unintended outcome. It also allowed us to project how the actions of others can influence our enactment. Including the voices of others made our narrative very realistic and practical. A map doesn't show a single path; it includes lots of places, some you may want to avoid. In constructing the narrative we want to happen, it is important that the paths we don't want to follow

are reflected as well. This helps us maintain focus and identify possible distractions or challenges before we encounter them. When we encounter challenges, we can act in a way that gets us back on track so we can enact our narrative and bring our vision to fruition. What we don't want to happen may be naturally implied in some cases, but being explicit helps. What we want to happen is not always the inverse of what we don't want to happen. On the defense team, within our plot to save our client's life, we constantly reflected the DA's plot—killing our client.

■ ■ ■

The first life we saved was Edwardo Garcia. Walter was Edwardo's attorney. He and I drove up to Milgram County to visit Edwardo in jail to inform him of a plea offer from the DA. The DA was willing to offer life without parole, but Edwardo had to agree. Walter could advise him, but the decision was up to Edwardo.

Two guards brought Edwardo into the small room and closed the steel door behind him. The guards left, leaving us locked in. The noise from the bolt echoed from deep inside six inches of heavy metal. The chains that shackled Edwardo's feet clinked across the cold cement floor as he shuffled toward us and sat across the table. I sat as far away from the table as I could that still qualified as being at the table, distracted by images of my own death. Maybe Edwardo would choke me with the very chains meant to protect me from him.

Walter leaned forward casually. Edwardo was dressed in a black-and-white striped jump suit that looked like it was designed by a cartoonist from the 1920s. I was shocked to learn that those uniforms really existed. Other prisoners wore orange jumpsuits, but black-and-white stripes signified the highest threat level. Prisoners in black and white had to be shackled at hand and foot and be escorted by at least two guards at all times.

Walter was making sure Edwardo understood his options given the plea offer, as well as trying to assess whether he was in fair enough mental health to be capable of making decisions. Edwardo had confided in us that he "heard voices."

"The voices don't say anything specific," Edwardo said, "they say stuff like, 'do it if you're gonna do it!' " he hissed through clinched teeth. His eyes darted left and right. Edwardo was reliving, not reporting, the voices.

"Are you hearing them right now?" Walter asked. He was interested in a strictly legal manner and was trying to determine Edwardo's competency to sign a plea tomorrow. I was interested in a "please don't let me ruin my pants" manner. My mind generated an increasingly creative and frightening mental list of what it might be that Edwardo was "gonna do if he was gonna do it."

"Nah," Edwardo assured us. "Not since that night."

"So you understand what you would be agreeing to?" Walter continued his legal checklist. "You understand you will never get out of prison? You will never even come up for parole."

During all of this, I was thinking half-heartedly, very nonchalantly, about chiming in to help Walter with the conversation, using all my effort to project an effortless cool and calm. I was also thinking about changing careers. The voices in my head were much more specific than Edwardo's. They said: "What are you doing here in this prison? Drop whatever brought you here. Get a different job. You could probably sell cars; something fancy, highbrow models, so you could still feel good about having gotten that stupid PhD. Heck, you could be sales manager one day." Somehow, through all that babbling, I was able to nod along reassuringly whenever Edwardo looked at me for a reaction to what Walter was advising—that he consider a sentence of life without parole instead of taking his chances at a death penalty trial in Texas.

As it turned out, the chains on Edwardo were completely unnecessary. He was remorseful about what he had done and reflexive about his future. Throughout the conversation, Edwardo was the kind person he had always been, not the person he was on the worst night of his life. The shackles served to remind us who we all were rather than to protect anyone.

Edwardo signed the plea agreement the next day in court. The victim's family gave Edwardo the victim's Bible. I am in awe of that kind of forgiveness.

On the long ride home from jail, Walter and I sat in the silence that only great relief brings. It was cathartic yet came with some anxiety. Our team had saved our first life, but dozens more already depended on our efforts. I also felt a deep sense of responsibility. If not knowing whether we could save lives by creating and enacting new narratives had tormented me, knowing we could, knowing we had, brought dread. We can stop executions.

Now we must. Because we can.

I reflected again on whether I chose this work or it chose me. I don't know. I do know that I was driven. How much choice that entails is anyone's guess.

It was late in the day as we left the courthouse. Edwardo was off to life in prison. Our narrative had worked. We had almost twenty cases, with more on the way. I reflected on the road ahead and felt the weight of the sun as it set. It turned the West Texas sky into a beautiful blaze of purple and orange. I started to mumble to Walter that I could never spend my life in a prison, but I stopped myself.

■ ■ ■

There are many kinds of prisons.

▪ ▪ ▪

I had been drunk for so long that I did not recognize myself when I quit. I didn't have any idea who I was without alcohol. I was a stranger to myself. I was uncomfortable and awkward in a sober body. Alcoholism can drive you to isolation, and those same urges for solitude followed me into sobriety. I still like to be alone, reluctant to engage in the world. My preference to become a hermit professor made my entry into the death penalty world a challenge. It was all new people and new contexts, a strange land. But the attraction of an adventure into the unknown garnered my interest. I was curious, and later I found a lot of meaning in the work of fighting the death penalty. I also still liked rebellion, but now I did it with purpose. I have said that if all of this was fate then fate could not have picked a more unlikely candidate. But later I began to believe this all might not be a mistake. I wondered if all my years of studying narratives, all the work I had done until then, even my rough experiences, maybe especially my rough experiences, had uniquely prepared me for this journey.

I am still making sense of it.

8
Narratives as a Way to Organize

Once you have constructed a new narrative, you need to enact it to bring its vision to reality. In this chapter, I describe what it takes to enact new narratives and the challenges to doing so. The situation is not as straightforward as you may think. Having managed to reorganize material in your stocks of knowledge to create a new narrative, your new way of doing things only exists as potential. You must be able to enact the new narrative to bring it into being. I also discuss what might help a new narrative become institutionalized, that is, widely shared and taken for granted enough to one day be "the ways things have always been done."

Many narratives may compete for enactment. In normal circumstances, we select a narrative that seems most appropriate to guide us through a particular situation. In making our narrative selection, we are pressured to reenact familiar narratives. This is our biggest challenge when enacting our new narrative. Not only are we extremely cautious when trying out a new narrative, but others also pressure us to stick to common scripts to accomplish routine interactions. For example, we all share an understanding of how a job interview should go. Everyone in that narrative has prescribed roles. There is a general implicit script: the interviewer describes the position, requirements, and needs; and the interviewee presents him- or herself as a match for the position. Our interactions go much more smoothly when we enact widely shared narratives and stick to the script.

We are rarely conscious that we are following a particular narrative, and we operate on autopilot much of the time. Even when we are aware that we are going by a narrative, we rarely question its legitimacy or underlying assumptions. All in all, that does not leave much space for new narratives, and even less opportunity for their enactment. Intentional narrative enactment takes a lot of reflexivity and conscientiousness.

What increases this potential? The new narrative must be salient, or be deemed appropriate given a particular situation. In a team setting, another way to increase enactment potential is for the team to explicitly agree to pursue narrative change as part of a formal process. This kind of buy-in requires an environment of trust.

It is crucial to be aware of the preexisting narratives operating in your field. You have to know industry history, for example, or be ready to respond to common scripts by offering an alternative narrative that is plausible. This is not an entirely new concept. For instance, good salespeople know their customers and are ready to respond to common reasons for not buying. Good salespeople have a stock of narratives to counteract those rationales.

The new narrative also has to work. Abductive thinking is needed to create a new narrative, but there is little forecasting or prediction when it comes to enacting an entirely new narrative. You just have to give the new concept a try. Put the narrative into action, and go by it, and see how things turn out. If it successfully guides you through that particular situation, it becomes more salient. Perhaps you have created a new narrative for how to manage product launches. If the launch goes well, you keep the new narrative.

Our death penalty defense team had agreed to co-create the narrative and then go by our new team narrative. But we also created strategic narratives for individual cases, and we used several scripts, or mini-narratives, to handle certain reoccurring situations. The more we encountered those situations and applied our new narratives to them, the more salient our narratives became. Some simple narratives became "go to" moves. Although our actions may have seemed counterintuitive to others, they were appropriate for our new way of seeing and doing things.

If your organization hopes to conduct transformational change, having a commitment to change up front greatly increases your chances of successful change. Second, it is important that key stakeholders from all levels in the organization participate in the narrative construction process. Including multiple voices and perspectives increases the likelihood that the new narrative will be representative of everyone involved with the organization.

Organizations that participate in this method of narrative construction benefit in a number of ways. Not only do they have a new narrative to go by, but the organization benefits from engaging in the construction process itself. Almost any type of team can benefit from co-creating a narrative they all agree to intentionally enact. Here are five benefits, but there are certainly others.

1. **A highly coordinated team is created.** Constructing the narrative together allows members to see their part in the whole organization in a clear, action-oriented way. The narrative provides a strategy that includes instructions about how to implement it. Team members have a sense and awareness of themselves, the team, and finally, of the self-in-team. As a result of collectively constructing a narrative, team members are able to envision and understand more clearly their role, the role of fellow team members, and most important, their role in relation to other team

members while enacting the narrative. Team members know their role as an individual and know the part their role plays in the entire organization. This allows members to predict the behavior of others as well as understand how their actions may affect others. Narrative enactment is proactive. Having a shared narrative increases the understanding of interactions, the reasons certain interactions occur, and what might be the next indicated actions not only for themselves but for fellow team members, given a multitude of contextual cues.

2. **Team members are empowered to act intelligently.** Team members may express a sense of being one step ahead in their work for the first time. Our team was better at predicting the cause and effect of their actions. There were fewer unintended consequences. When enacting a new narrative, team members know they are going by a shared narrative they collectively constructed, which empowers them to act with confidence. Throughout the process of constructing the narrative, team members were required to take the role of the other in considering the effects of their actions and projecting the reactions of others, including outsiders, such as the DA. For our team, those projections became story lines that we incorporated into the narrative.

3. **Individuals improvise flexibly, quickly, and proactively.** Having a collective narrative enables informed individual improvisation. Team members can improvise as well as predict the effects of their improvisations. It gives them flexibility during enactment, allowing them to account for situational particularities while still acting to bring the team narrative to fruition through their actions. Team members know where they fit into the story and are able to make snap decisions about how best to move the narrative forward. They can improvise actions that make things easier for others down the line, and they see

options and can play them out (follow actions through likely consequences). Everyone on the team is action-oriented yet highly flexible at the same time. Of course, going by the same narrative means they can accurately interpret the improvisations of others. The sentiment is: "You know what we are trying to do, and you are free to take actions that will make that happen." Again, it takes, but also creates, trust.

4.   **A freethinking space is created that enables change.** The narrative construction process is a reflexive act. Team members surface and gain an awareness of their own assumptions and norms, critiquing each of them. They are able to put each assumption up for review, and they recall how that assumption came into place or how it might be deconstructed. If, for example, a norm is still strongly held but the original reason for it is long gone, the team can jettison or modify this assumption. The narrative construction process invokes a freethinking space about future prospects instead of restricting thinking to what is "allowed" under current norms. Narrative construction and enactment is free from a lot of the constraints of normative pressure. These reflexive, critical insights take some hard work, but they enable tremendous change.

5.   **Shared understanding creates a strong culture.** Creating a collective narrative creates a strong culture. Organizational culture is a shared understanding about values and the way things should be done. People develop shared understandings out of shared experiences. Creating a narrative is a shared experience that *also* produces a shared understanding.

■ ■ ■

Let's take a moment to consider how awareness of the narrative selection process can help you predict, and maybe even influence, the narrative selection of others; that is, what they go by during an interaction. On our team, we became aware of the narratives we were enacting, but we tried to be aware of the narratives others might enact in particular situations as well.

I like to think of narratives as little clouds overhead, and the narrative currently directing our actions as the most salient cloud, that is, the one that seems most appropriate or relevant for a particular situation. District attorneys, for example, are pressured to conform to many narratives. When we first meet the DA, the usual narrative is one we might call "seek justice." If the DA is guided by that narrative, and manages to enact it, our client gets killed at the end. But other narratives are hovering in the cognitive skies over the DA's head. For instance, the DA is an elected official and is worried about budgets and how much taxpayer money should be spent. So somewhere in the DA's cognitive framework is another narrative called the "reduce spending" narrative. Our strategy is to act in such a way that the reduce spending narrative becomes more salient than the seek justice narrative. We attempt to influence which narrative the DA "goes by."

We want to make the DA change the narrative he or she selects. To do this, we enact one of our narratives called "increase the cost of a case." The DA's reduce spending narrative then becomes more salient and a more appropriate narrative to select for enactment. In enacting a narrative we choose, we are signaling which narrative *they* should choose to go by. Of course, it has to be one we know is already in their cognitive structure.

This is by no means a secret strategy. In fact, you may be aware that increasing the cost of a case is common, and absolutely proper, in many legal settings. The defense team can prove the need for many types of experts, and the DA knows that for every expert we put on they will need another to counter their testimony. The costs are legitimate, and they can mount quickly. We may need our client tested to see if exposure to lead paint as a child damaged the area of the brain that controls behavioral impulse. The money for all these extra expenses, which are required for putting on a fair defense, and to which the client is entitled under due process, comes from the courts—ultimately from the taxpayers. We file funding motions to the judge, who knows that any denial of funds necessary to put on a defense in a death penalty case will be highly scrutinized by appellate courts. If our requests are denied, the appeals courts may find we were not provided the due process the Constitution requires.

The judge is loath to give us the money, but at the same time is wary to deny us. The cost of a case can quickly skyrocket. If we can drive the cost up enough, the DA becomes reluctant to keep raising the stakes and folds. Eventually, the DA may shift attention to the reduce spending narrative. If we can get the DA to go by that narrative, enacting it will save money and resolve the case before all these requested expenditures occur—by offering us a plea.

This points to one problem with DAs being elected officials. Although they certainly pursue justice, they also pursue reelection. I'll let you contemplate which is their top concern. Under these pressures, DAs are forced to make politically motivated decisions, not only justice decisions. DAs often do what's popular, not what's right. Given the focus on money that goes along with being an elected official nowadays, they are incentivized to pursue cases that are relatively inexpensive to prosecute. Given their professional reputations, there are incentives only to pursue cases that are easy to win, and to make the hard or expensive ones go away.

It is helpful to know the narratives others are likely to have among their cognitive frameworks. You may be aware of industry norms, for example, or common reasons customers do or do not buy a product or service. By knowing the narratives from which they will choose, you can act to signal, or cue, a particular narrative as being the most applicable to the situation. You can influence others to select a narrative whose enactment results in an outcome more favorable to you.

After two years, the office was garnering lots of attention in government circles. We had won many awards, but the most prestigious was Best Public Safety Office in the country. At that point, we had stopped more than thirty executions. We had not lost a case. In winning the award, we beat every other public health and safety office in the country, including every police, fire, and first responder department. We got the award because local governments were impressed with the amount of taxpayer money we saved while making quality improvements to the justice system. Every time we stopped an execution, we saved taxpayers a ton of money. In fact, we had won so many awards that Walter asked people over in the commissioner's office to quit nominating us. "If we win any more awards," Walter said, "we'll go broke!"

The new office did not have any funds budgeted to travel to collect all the awards we had won. Winning the Best Public Safety Office award meant Walter would have to travel to Nashville to accept it and have his picture taken with someone by a podium while holding a plaque. This award was prestigious enough that Walter had to go, but because we had no money, Walter used his own airline miles to get there and paid for a hotel out of his own pocket.

We were also benefiting from our reputation as a hardworking team. The effect was difficult to track, but we had anecdotal evidence that district attorneys were avoiding filing capital murder charges just so they would not have to face us.

One DA called Walter asking for help. He wanted it both ways—the DA wanted to file capital murder charges (and therefore maintain his tough on crime bona fides) but not face us. Walter was happy to help him. He assured the DA that we only took cases in which the defendant actually faced the death penalty. Walter further instructed him, "What you can do is go ahead and file capital charges as usual, but then the next day you file a motion waiving death as a penalty." This move happened on many of our cases, but it was rare to get a call from an inexperienced DA asking how it all worked.

Waiving death turns a capital case into what is called a "mini-cap," short for miniature capital case. It signified that capital charges were being brought, but death would not be sought in the punishment phase. In those trials, if the defendant was found guilty of capital murder in the first phase of the trial, there was no second phase, or sentencing hearing. The judge entered a sentence of life without parole.

The DA would still get to be on the front page of the local newspaper, and the newspaper could rightly print "DA seeks Capital Murder Charges." The DA could tell everyone he stuck to his tough on crime campaign promises by filing capital murder charges, but he also avoided facing us by waiving death as a penalty. Having "Capital Murder Charges" blasted across the front page of the local newspaper kept the DA's political future safe. The news about death being waived never made the papers. Instead of facing us, the DA would face the same old familiar local court-appointed attorneys, attorneys who still faced all the pressures of getting along to go along and stood a good chance of being more deferential to the judge.

"So if I file that motion," the DA asked, "you guys won't be appointed on the case?"

"That's right," said Walter.

"What exactly goes into one of these motions to dismiss death as a penalty?"

"I'll send you one over," said Walter.

At night, if I did manage to sleep, I would gnaw at my fingernails until they bled. Defending the damned and being exposed to horrific crime scenes and facts continued to wear on my psyche.[1] I was conflicted by all the same questions people always asked death penalty defense attorneys. "How can you do this work?" they ask, or "Why would you defend someone like that?"

One pat answer is that everyone has human rights. In the appeals process, defendants can waive almost all of their rights, but they can never waive their constitutional rights. People often find this astounding. You can guess what they say.

"Look at what they've done! They don't deserve any rights."

My answer is that rights are not something we give out based on whether or not we find people deserving. You'd better pray that never becomes the case (again). Rights are something we all have, and something we defend for others, not because of what doing so says *about them* but because of what it says *about us*.

Finally, as a moral principle, no matter what you've done, no matter how bad you have been, you can never stop being human. I could have used this advice myself. There were times in my life when I did not feel very human, and it made the road back much harder.

One evening after I had presented at a seminar for defense attorneys, I sat chatting in a lobby with iconic death penalty defense attorney Millard Farmer. He had practiced in Georgia and took on black clients at a time when it was very unpopular. Typically, black defendants were appointed black attorneys, and defendants were subsequently railroaded to death row by judges and prosecutors who gave little attention to a fair trial.

Millard offended people in two ways. First, he took black clients facing the death penalty. Second, he tried very hard to defend them. In doing so, he lost many of his friends and faced constant death threats. Millard created a narrative called "conflictioneering." He continuously questioned the normal way things were done in the death penalty, and he not only critiqued those narratives but acted to introduce conflict at every turn. His aim was to make it harder and harder for judges and prosecutors to kill his clients. Millard threw as many wrenches as he could into the machinery of death. Millard resisted those old narratives and enacted his conflictioneering narrative. It made people mad. DAs and judges threatened to have him disbarred. The KKK once firebombed a house he was staying at during a trial.

Millard had a good sense of humor about the cost of his convictions. "I'm the only attorney I know who had to show up to court in the trunk of his car!" he joked. Lots of people thought Millard had as much chance of being killed as his clients.

Millard asked me how I was doing. He had heard about our success in Lubbock. "As you know better than I, it can be tough work," I told him. "I have my doubts about how long I can stick with it." I was asking him his reason for doing this at all costs.

"The Constitution is in the Smithsonian," Millard said. "It's just sitting there. It doesn't do a damn thing on its own. We have to make it speak. And if we can't make it speak for the worst of us, then it cannot speak for the best of us."

That night I slept like a baby.

■ ■ ■

My chest burned and I gasped for air as I entered the courthouse. Five minutes beforehand I had bounded out of the business school and sprinted across the parking lot. Seconds before that, I was in the middle of a lecture when I got a text message from Robin: We have a verdict.

Robin was staying in my downstairs guest room for the length of the Seth Rose trial. When she texted me that a verdict was in, I ran out of the classroom. I might have told my class we were finished for the day, or I might have just started running. As I reached my car, fumbling for my keys, I dropped the dry erase marker that was still in my hand.

As I entered the courtroom, the only noise came from the creaking wooden benches as people adjusted themselves in the gallery. The crowd spilled into the hallways, but people on the defense team had saved my usual seat in the front row on the aisle.

There were extra bailiffs in the courtroom to provide a show of force while the verdict was read. The biggest bailiff was a six-foot eight-inch, egg-shaped mound of man who was planted in front of the banister that cut the courtroom in half. He towered over the gallery but made no eye contact.

People stood suddenly. The judge had emerged from his chambers.

"Please be seated," the judge said. "When I read the verdict, there will be no outburst or commentary. This has been a long process. We have kept decorum and will continue to do so." He nodded to a deputy standing by the door near the jury box. Everyone stood again as the jury shuffled in, the first six down the back row, and the next six in the front row, taking the same seats they had taken for almost a hundred days now.

As always, I studied them intently. This time was different. It was the last time they would enter the box. They all knew that, and they were the only ones who knew whether Seth Rose had been sentenced to death. The sentencing deliberations had gone on for two days. The guilty verdict had been fast and was no surprise. In fact, Seth had begun the trial by entering a guilty plea, but the prosecution still put on their entire case. Already sentenced to two consecutive life without parole terms in Arkansas, there was no upside to staging a defense. Guilt was not a question, so it had been conceded from the start. The entire trial was about killing or saving Seth, so the team had put all their efforts into the sentencing phase.

"Mr. Foreman, it is my understanding that you have reached a verdict?" the judge asked.

"Yes, Your Honor."

The bailiff took an envelope from the foreman and walked across the courtroom and handed it to the judge. The judge opened it and turned through several pages, then back to the first. He began to read.

"On count one, with regard to special issue number one, you have found unanimously that the defendant poses a future danger to commit continuing acts of criminal violence."

"Yes, Your Honor."

"On count one, with regard to special issue number two as to mitigating circumstances, you were unable to reach a consensus."

"Yes, Your Honor."

"On count two, with regard to special issue number one, you have found unanimously that the defendant poses a future danger to commit continuing acts of criminal violence."

The judge read on placidly, going through all three counts, one for each of Seth's victims, reading the pages methodically for the record. But it was over. From that point on, I could have recited it myself. Every count was the same. The jury did not reach an agreement on the mitigation questions.

I looked around and until I caught someone's eye. Larry Calvert, a mitigator on our team, gave me the slightest nod by dropping his chin. Disbelief rushed through me. Robin sat dumbfounded. When her eyes met mine, they widened and her mouth opened slightly.

The guys at the defense table sat solemnly. Seth showed no emotion. The courtroom remained quiet. We remained nearly frozen, although everyone on the defense team knew this meant that Seth would be sentenced to life without parole.

Of the many feelings I had, one was a sense of relief, but only the type of relief you feel when a bullet barely misses you.

Awestruck by the ongoing silence, I turned to look at the victim's family on the other side of the gallery. I could have told you who was sitting where before I looked. We had never exchanged a word, but they had seen me come and go every day in court, scribbling for hours on end in my yellow notepad. They always sat in the same places too. They saw me constantly talking with the defense team. They noticed when Seth would wave to me. We were constantly and mutually aware of one another, but we never spoke or made eye contact.

They had exchanged perplexed looks with one another at an earlier time when Andy Thomas, one of Seth's attorneys, had burst into the back of the courtroom just before court started. "Professor! Professor!" he called in a stage whisper, crouching low and waving frantically for me to follow him into the hall for some last minute strategizing. Court had been called into session by the bailiff, but the judge had not yet entered. As I briskly exited, the victim's family and friends had stared at each other in confusion about what was happening.

They looked that way now.

I am still filled with pity for the family. My insides dropped, like someone had cut the bottom out of a sack and sent the contents rushing to the floor. In a few minutes, the judge would announce that he was required by law to enter a sentence of life without parole. For the first time, their faces would show faint signs of recognition about what was happening. Seth would live.

■ ■ ■

At the time of this writing, Uber's future is yet to be determined. They will need to make major changes if they hope to thrive. The report on the company culture from Eric Holder gives an indication of the old narratives and some recommended changes, but it exists as a list, not a narrative. The Holder report on Uber is made up of forty-seven bullet points, but as I have said, what is needed is deeper than bullet points. Bullet points don't come with an implementation plan. A lot of the changes the Holder report recommends are new positions and responsibility, creating a more independent board of directors, and performance reviews to address some of the issues. There are only a few suggestions about changing the culture at Uber. The Holder report calls for an emphasis on teamwork, collaboration, and even joy. This is a nice list, but a list leaves a lot to be fleshed out. Remember, a narrative entails not only a goal but an actionable way to get there. You can't enact a list. Uber needs a narrative they can enact, one where employees can see themselves as part of the plot and know what concrete actions are required to move the narrative plot to their desired ends.

Constructing a narrative can bring the list into an actionable script that employees can enact in their everyday interactions at work. A new narrative at Uber could model the new cultural values and also serve as the tool for their implementation.

Ubers's new CEO, Dara Khosrowshahi, seems willing to change. He is not quiet about Uber's past mistakes. Uber settled several lawsuits that threatened to further tarnish Uber's reputation before Khosrowshahi became CEO, including a $10 million lawsuit brought on behalf of women and minority engineers who claimed they were paid less than white male equals.

Uber insiders note that there is already a new saying around the corporate offices: "No jerks allowed, no matter how brilliant." Khosrowshahi has also suggested eight new cultural values at Uber that encourage the celebration of differences, customer focus, bold bets, and the importance of new ideas. I have already seen one of these values in a series of TV commercials: Do the right thing.

To create a new narrative at Uber, management could have a key group from all levels of the organization flesh out exactly what doing the right thing might entail, especially when doing the right thing may reduce profit or productivity. The narrative should show employees what new types of actions are engendered by a do the right thing narrative. It would provide a template of expectations and give employees the flexibility to do the right thing in a variety of situations. As for goals, a narrative would provide a strategy on steroids—not only a big goal but a plan for how to bring it to fruition.

If Uber cannot imagine what do the right thing looks like in a narrative, or exactly how growth will be achieved, what chance do they have of enacting it in everyday operations? If Uber wants a new values-based narrative to become institutionalized and replace the old way of doing things, it will have to be salient to employees, customers, and all stakeholders. The new narrative has to be widely shared and frequently enacted. I would suggest that Uber create a series of doing the right thing stories that show how Uber enacts its new core value. They could capture and share successful enactments of their new narrative.

A new narrative will have to achieve some other things to become the new way things are done around Uber. First, it has to work. The new narrative has to successfully help the company navigate some previously difficult situations. Employees have to use it to interact in new ways. Narrative enactment is a pragmatic test. The narrative has to make itself useful in application. Second, the new narrative has to gain legitimacy. People have to see that everyone in the organization is going by the new narrative and doing the right thing. This will make the old ways, like internal backstabbing, less and less legitimate.

9
A Narrative for You

This chapter is for you. You can use the change model immediately to develop your own personal leadership narrative. You do not need to be a CEO or be in charge of a large-scale organizational transformation to apply the narrative change model. You can start right now, in your own life. I explain how to apply the narrative change model to your own life to change something about yourself or to attain personal career goals.

In my executive MBA courses, I help managers create personal leadership narratives. Having guidelines to draw on and go by gives them direction and ideas on how they might progress in their careers. It is also a map they can turn to in times of crisis or when navigating crucial moments. Personal narratives keep them on track. Having a personal leadership narrative to go by aids their decision-making at work, empowers them to act, and gives them confidence in doing so. Several people have also reported significant personal transformations. They tell me that in developing a leadership narrative they have finally found a path. I remind them that they created this path, maybe where it did not exist before.

Developing a personal leadership model requires two broad steps. As you might guess by now, we first have to become aware of any current narratives that may be constraining our potential. For example, a very old narrative, but one I still encounter occasionally in undergraduate classes, says that women do not make good leaders. I am afraid it may be more widespread than we would like to think, and worse, I believe too many people still go by this narrative when making decisions and interpretations.

Asking questions about a narrative's origin begins the deconstruction. Who created it? What purpose did it serve? Who benefits from that narrative? We know that all narratives are socially constructed. The idea that women don't make good leaders is the product of a male-dominated society interested in retaining leadership positions for themselves to the exclusion of all others. Research does not support the narrative that women don't make good leaders, but as I have stressed several times now, the truth of a narrative has nothing to do with whether it becomes institutionalized. The assumptions instilled by a narrative will exist as long as the narrative is continuously enacted.

Maintaining the status quo is not about inaction. Old narratives don't stick around because we don't do anything about them. They stick around because we continue to enact them. It takes constant reconstruction to keep old narratives around. Maintaining the status quo is not passive; it takes a lot of effort.

Narratives are creations that become true; they are made up and then made real. That fact has positive and negative aspects. On the negative side, narratives are independent of truth and can be made real through enactment. On the positive side, we can create a vision for ourselves and act it into being.

Becoming aware of the narratives that constrain us requires self-reflection. At one time, I could not imagine my life without alcohol. Even when I knew it was killing me, it was unlikely that I would ever give it up. My narrative said alcohol made me comfortable when I felt like I did not fit in anywhere. That narrative kept me clutching onto something that was hurting me. I thought drinking smoothed out all of the rough edges in the world—but all the rough edges were on me, not on the world. I thought it made my life bigger, when in fact my life had become very, very small. At the end, there was nothing in my life but booze. I was either drunk or waiting to get drunk.

One narrative I found helpful in recovery was to "get outside of yourself." In enacting it, I tried to get over my feelings of wanting to isolate by contributing to something, anything other than my own self-interest. That narrative left no room to wallow in pain or self-pity or to try to remedy any of it with a drink. There was no way to wish it to happen, and it was not a contemplation exercise. I had to act by getting outside of myself. I had to be of service, which certainly made me feel better, perhaps just because I put my focus elsewhere instead of obsessing over alcohol. At first, the notion that doing something for someone else could benefit me seemed a bit mysterious. I was self-centered in the extreme. I also know I am not the only one. Getting outside of myself also may have tricked me into seeing that I had something to offer. Whenever I enact that narrative, I am better for it.

Interestingly, a management theory called stakeholder theory includes some of these ideas. Stakeholder theory stands in juxtaposition to traditional thinking about a corporation's duty to please its shareholders—the owners of the firm. Shareholders are one of a firm's stakeholders, but a list of all stakeholders goes beyond shareholders to include a concern for customers, suppliers, the communities in which the firm operates, and more. A stakeholder is anyone affected by the operations of the firm. If you try to improve the lives of all your stakeholders—not just the shareholders—you do much better than if you focus solely on shareholders, which is the traditional narrative.

This theory offers the possibility of a new narrative. What if a firm focused on improving the lives of their customers? That firm would probably have devoted customers who were willing to pay premium prices because their lives are being improved. And what would the firm get out of it? Lots of customers, and the bottom line would probably improve more than it would if they focused only on improving the bottom line. Why should a corporation go out of its way to improve things for their suppliers? One outcome of a healthy supplier is that you have insured top quality inputs to your products. You also help maintain the ecosystem you depend on for your survival.

"What do you think happens to profits?" I ask my students.

"They go up?"

"Yes," I say, "some research suggests that the more firms take this perspective, the better they do in the long run."

The logic is that if you focus on making things better and better for stakeholders, your own success increases as a side effect.

■ ■ ■

I often ask executive students to engage in a thought experiment inspired by enacting the stakeholder narrative at a personal level. I ask them to imagine devoting themselves solely to improving the lives of their friends instead of their own. I tell them to identify a circle of twelve friends and to think about how it would all play out if they completely devoted their lives to improving the lives of these friends. What would happen?

Maybe one wants to learn French. Take a class with her, or get a program and sit with her for an hour a day, making sure you both learn. Perhaps another wants to get into shape and eat healthy. To ensure his success, you wake up at 5 A.M. every day and lead him through a boot camp style workout. Another friend of yours wants to lead her region in medical device sales. You set goals with her every week and help her achieve them. You listen to and craft her sales pitch to customers. You not only encourage her to follow up after sales visits but make a spreadsheet and tick off tasks for her. Together you explore new markets and brainstorm sales strategies to reach new customers.

Perhaps another wants to pass the Series 7 exam and become a licensed stock trader. Another wants to be CEO of her company in five years.

"Okay," I say, "that's only five of the twelve friends you are helping, but let's assume you will be very busy helping the other seven people in the same fashion. Your only goal is to help them achieve their goals, doing whatever that takes. This is your new personal narrative, and you are able to enact it time and time again. What would happen?"

"They'd suck you dry," someone laughs.

"Their lives would get better and better," says another quickly. "You would probably have some friends in high places."

"Yes," says the first, "their lives would be great, but what about you?"

"You'd be a badass," someone else calls out. "Think about it. If you did all the stuff in just these examples, you would have learned another language, be in awesome shape, and have some pretty powerful corporate skills."

"So *you* would be better off," I say, "and you would have all these accomplished friends. Do you think you would have any trouble finding a job? If your friends were not great connections before, you have turned them into great connections, and I bet they would be willing to help you. Remember, these are friends you helped, not strangers."

"It would work," claims a student.

"I think so," I say. "You have to think of yourselves as all tied together, and if you help them rise, you get pulled up too. To go even further, if you devoted your life to improving the lives of others, your life would be the most improved of all."

There are slow nods.

"So what is stopping us?" I continue. "If we genuinely believe this to be true, and if we would benefit the most, why wouldn't we live according to this narrative? If I told you it was all guaranteed, how many of you would do it?"

Not one hand. They exchange grimaces.

"Me neither," I confide. "Even though I believe it is true. Even though I am absolutely positive that my own life would improve tenfold if I improved the lives of others, I still am unable to do it. It really is a mystery to me."

What I don't tell them is that it is worse for me, even hypocritical, because I know from experience that it works. On the few occasions I have gotten outside of myself and helped others, the results were nothing but positive. The simple act of doing something for someone else kept me sober when nothing else would. I know my struggle indicates I have many character defects and lots of work to do. I am still too selfish and self-centered. But I can enact this narrative any time. I can try it more and more often, aspiring to progress rather than perfection.

I did not provide this story to suggest that it is the narrative for you, especially when I struggle to enact it myself. I only use it as an example—your own narrative must resonate deeply with you.

■ ■ ■

I do have some suggestions for developing your own personal narrative. The narrative construction steps are the same as those presented in chapter 8 for building organizational narratives, but there are some other aspects to highlight.

Recall that first we have to expose and deconstruct any narratives that may be constraining us. Perhaps you have something in your cognitive framework that is controlling you. It may be a self-imposed limitation. You can get better at deconstruction of detrimental narratives by critiquing every narrative you enact. Think of any structures, including some you may not be fully aware of, and how they control you. One way to surface controlling narratives is to become hyperconscious of mundane daily actions. Examine everything you do and ask yourself why; this can reveal what you are going by. Have you recently avoided a confrontation? Why was that?

Consider the left side of the change model where narrative structures control our actions, behaviors, and interpretations, pressuring us to act in habitual ways. Speaking for myself, I rarely send food back at restaurants, no matter how much they mess up my order. That narrative includes assumptions about not wanting to make a fuss or be a bother and, of course, the fear many of us share—they will do bad things to my food in the kitchen if I send it back. Next I ask where I got the narrative about not wanting to make a fuss. When did I start to go by this narrative? I was most likely socialized to not make a fuss. Perhaps as a child I witnessed several encounters where someone was apologetic about pointing out a mistake. I am sure I heard the rumor "they'll spit in your food" when I was a teenager, and it was probably my own shortcomings that made it seem plausible. The result of this narrative is that I never send food back for fear of making a fuss or even retribution from the kitchen. Upon reflection, nothing really supports these assumptions. There is nothing wrong with wanting your order to be correct. I do not need to feel bad about it, and to be honest, the "fuss"

I am worried about making is probably next to nothing to most restaurants. They would probably rather I was happy and came back than be disappointed in silence and not give them a chance to easily correct a mistake. Maybe they serve thousands of chicken sandwiches and won't really be offended if I point out that the one they made for my daughter should not have come with pickles. I think asking for another chicken sandwich is some big imposition, but it is likely that they could not care less.

Practice makes us better at discovering narratives we go by and how they influence our actions. Deconstructing those narratives gives us a chance to create new ones, or at the very least to quit enacting narratives that constrain us. I encourage you to think of specific narratives that you follow. Reflect on your own actions and critique why you engage in any practice. Where did you get that narrative? How did it get into your head, your cognitive structure? Is it valid? Or is it just a habit? Did you just adopt it from someone else? It may have been made up for a reason, but is that reason still legitimate? How does it influence your actions? What is the result for you?

As you deconstruct narratives and their assumptions, you open space to create new narratives. When developing a personal narrative, make it as action-oriented as possible. You must be able to enact your narrative. You could start by exploring your own convictions. What is important to you? Is there something you believe in deeply? What are you passionate about?

Think of three things that make you happy or mad. What fills you with joy or drives you up the wall? Pair each of your convictions with an aspiration. What do you want to achieve or accomplish? In exploring this question, ask who has inspired you and how. Think of three traits, characteristics, or behaviors that you like in others. (Hint, these will become aspirations to narrate for yourself.)

Next, think of how you might accomplish your aspirations. This prepares you for thinking about actions that will lead to achieving your aspirations. What tools do you have at your disposal? When have you successfully faced a challenge? What did you rely on to get you through it? What are you good at? When have you felt like you were "in the zone" and performing at a high level, and what were you doing? How were you acting? What was allowing you to keep it going? What are three "weapons" that you have in your character or skill set? How did you use any of them to overcome a challenge? For example, maybe you play a good devil's advocate during decision-making. Did you save your team from making a bad decision? I am good at turning conventional wisdom on its head and looking at old problems in new ways. I have to practice this skill often, and seeing things in new ways has helped me deconstruct controlling narratives.

Finally, think of how you can use your "weapons" to pursue your aspirations while maintaining your convictions. What does using your weapons look like? Are you able to get people to voice their opinion when they are hesitant to do so? Do you have a knack for making people feel comfortable? What actions bring your aspirations to fulfillment?

Write a narrative about your aspirations becoming true in story format. You have a vision of where you want to go, now list the concrete steps you will take to get there. What actions will result in your next promotion? What time do you get up in the morning? What do you do next? When a customer makes a demand, how do you react? Think of a hypothetical scene in which a customer complains, and script your reaction.

For broader elements, what does it look like when you stick to your convictions? For example, if it is important to you as a leader that everyone is heard and feels that they are heard, can you construct a narrative of what that looks like? Do you have meetings with employees before making any decision that affects them rather than informing them of decisions already made?

Give others a voice in your personal narrative. As you are acting to achieve your goals, what are other people around you doing? When you ask for your followers' input, what happens to it? Do subordinates see that their input was considered and included? Going by such a leadership narrative can be challenging.

■ ■ ■

Uber and I share a narrative. One of the first narratives I recall attempting to enact was a simple one, and coincidently it is the exact same narrative Uber is focusing on now: Do the right thing. For both Uber and me, there is nothing wrong with a basic narrative, especially if we have fallen far. When you are starting from the bottom, like I was, a basic narrative helps keep it simple.

When I was less than a year sober, I found a wallet in New York City and went to extraordinary lengths to return it, surprising myself. The wallet had lots of money in it. I was a graduate student at the time, so even a small amount of money was a lot to me, but this would have been a lot of money to anyone. I was still clearing the wreckage of my recent past, and that money would have solved a lot of problems for me.

Previously I would have quickly evoked the narrative "finder's keepers," taken the money, and solved an array of pressing problems. This time, with great difficulty, I half-heartedly, regretfully, resentfully, and against my usual judgment decided to try to do the right thing.

I found the wallet in Barneys on Madison Avenue, a high-end retail store (I was just ogling price tags), and I knew the owner might still be there. I asked the staff to make an announcement over the PA system, but they refused. "We can stick it in that lost and found box over there," a salesperson suggested apathetically. I just knew this guy would never see his wallet again if that happened.

I left with the wallet and went to a coffee shop. I found a small stack of identical cards in the wallet listing a Washington, D.C. office, which I deduced must have been the owner's. I got his assistant on the phone and tried to explain that I needed to reach him. She kept interrupting me to tell me that her boss was not available and she could not give out his personal cell phone number. He was in New York.

"I know," I said, "I have his wallet. I'm in New York."

We went back and forth several times before she made sense of what was happening. I eventually got his cell phone number and called to tell him I had his wallet. He was some kind of diplomat from Central America. "I haven't lost my w—," he stopped himself. I could hear him patting himself down. He was in a cab on the way to the airport, and we arranged to meet on a street corner in Manhattan. When he showed up, he looked dumbfounded, staring at me like he was trying to solve a puzzle. I handed him his wallet and he immediately stuffed it in his front coat pocket.

"I want to buy you a nice dinner or something, but I am late getting to the airport already."

I told him that was not necessary.

"Will I make my flight?" he suddenly asked me, looking at his watch. It was not a rhetorical question. He really seemed to be relying on me now.

"Why not?" I said, "You're having a great day." I went to pat his shoulder, but he came in for a big, gregarious bear hug. At the time, I needed that more than a nice dinner.

The cab was halfway down the street when it screeched to a halt. He threw open the door, stuck his face out, and yelled, "Hans! I didn't know that people like you existed!" He was flapping his wallet at me. The cash stack visible in the billfold.

Me neither, I thought. This definitely was not me, but it felt great. I planned on being "not me" a lot more. If I kept enacting do the right thing, maybe it would become the real me. I could choose to enact the better image of myself more often. It could become me.

That experience changed my assumptions about doing the right thing, which I had always thought of as some kind of burden. However costly it is to do what is right, the return is always better. You are not doing the right thing just because it makes others feel great. You are doing the right thing because it makes you feel great.

▪ ▪ ▪

Today I have a leadership narrative that I try to go by as often as I can. Not only do I use it to direct my actions and aspire to its ideas, I use my narrative for self-motivation. It was built from my personal experience, my death penalty defense work, and some reflections and realizations inspired by others—characteristics I see in others that I aspire to in myself.

My own narrative consists of two parts. The first part is a conviction/aspiration to "speak for those who cannot speak for themselves." This narrative emerged from and resonated with me during my death penalty defense work; our team spoke for people when no one else would. We never considered whether our clients were deserving of our efforts. When we protect others, we don't ask whether they are deserving. It is not just about them. We were deserving of our ideals. We don't help others because of who they are; we help others because of who we are. Of course, it is influenced from my experience in recovery as well, and it allows me to "get outside of myself." Enacting this narrative has confirmed for me that I am the biggest benefactor in doing something for someone else.

The second part of my personal narrative is a constant challenge to myself. It comes in the form of a reflexive question: "Can you do it when it's hard?" Whatever we aspire to, can we maintain our resolve when it is difficult to do so? For example, I can exercise when I feel great, but can I do it when I feel disinterested? I like making time for family, but does it remain a priority when I am overwhelmed with projects at work? And sure, I can give away half of my sandwich when I am not hungry, but can I give it away when I am starving? Can I do it when it's hard?

This narrative was inspired by something someone said. It was nothing more than an offhand comment to him, but it was a significant moment for me. I was teaching in Europe a few summers ago and went to Greece for the weekend. On my way to the airport, the taxi I was in passed several makeshift refugee camps. Refugees from Syria and other war-torn countries had been pouring into Greece to escape persecution and starvation. People were overloading boats and risking their lives to cross the Mediterranean or Aegean Sea to land somewhere in Greece to enter the European Union and start life over. Greece set up dozens of refugee camps to house the hundreds of thousands of immigrants who made the perilous journey. The refugees arrived hungry, tired, and weak. These huddled masses needed food, clothes, and shelter. Providing for them took enormous resources. It was a worldwide humanitarian crisis, but Greece shouldered much of the burden. On top of all this, Greece had been in a severe financial crisis before the refugees arrived. Almost a third of the country was unemployed. Greece had massive debt and was unable to make payments, even with dramatic increases in taxes and deep spending cuts. The economy was on the verge of collapse. There was a run on the banks and riots in the streets.

So I asked my taxi driver, "How can Greece afford to help these people?" This is a narrative we hear a lot in the United States. We do not want to help others; we have our own problems. Why are we spending all this money on others when we have our own needs at home?

The driver did not hesitate. "Because it's the right thing to do!" he threw his arms up.

"But Greece is broke!" I said.

He shrugged it off. "It's the right thing to do when you're rich, and it's the right thing to do when you're poor."

■ ■ ■

I have combined my conviction to speak for those who cannot speak for themselves and my aspiration to do it when it is hard into a guiding leadership narrative. I seek ways to speak for those who cannot speak for themselves, even when, especially when, it is hard. I come up short many times, but having a narrative to go by directs my efforts and motivates me. It helps me attain some of my more aspirational stretch goals, which are more difficult to reach. Having too many stretch goals can be demotivating, but have some—stretching keeps you limber.

10
Big Ideas and Narrative Modes

reating leadership narratives for yourself is a valuable endeavor, but I have not forgotten my promise to you that new narratives can have a larger impact—they can change the world. The same narrative change model is applied when considering large-scale change programs, but it is paramount that the narrative resonates with a much broader audience. This is no small task. To be transformative, any new narrative, vision, or way of seeing something must become widely shared and enacted. It has to go viral, to use today's terms, and inspire people to bring the narrative to fruition through enactment.

Let's take on the grand collective challenge of our time as an example: climate change. Despite widespread agreement in the scientific community, our current approach to climate change is not working. I implore everyone to recognize that the solution must be socially as well as scientifically oriented. What resonates with people may have little relation to the facts. Our current narrative has not led to enactment. Facts are fickle, and no amount of scientific facts alone will inspire people to act. Climate change denial, which has no basis in fact, resonates with many people. Facts alone do not motivate action; it takes more than facts.

To inspire action around climate change, we need a new narrative. Powerful (and incorrect) narratives already reside in this context, so we face a huge challenge on the social front. Too many people have adopted one of these two narratives: climate change is not happening or climate change is natural and out of our control. Both narratives inspire a do nothing stance. Much to the consternation of the scientific community, the narrative that we must enact to reduce climate change offers a conceptual framework that is too easily dismissed, rejected, or, perhaps most damaging, ignored. The current narrative of climate change is too abstract. The competing assumptions around this debate cannot be resolved. If we are waiting for climate change alarmists and climate change deniers to come to an agreement, we will die waiting. We need an entirely new framework within which to act.

I have pondered a new narrative framing climate change as "pollution." I might go so far as recommending that we quit saying "climate change" all together to avoid drawing attention to that impasse. Society has a shared narrative, and a collective understanding, about pollution and how it should be addressed. At a basic level, we all agree that pollution should be reduced. It is a taken for granted and unquestioned assumption—pollution is something we want to reduce. Not only do we share this deeply rooted assumption, nobody argues about whether pollution is real. When people discuss pollution, the debate is always about solutions—which ones to pursue, which ones will work— and not whether the pursuit is warranted. Our shared social narrative regarding pollution already has legitimacy and nearly complete social acceptance. Pollution is caused by humans and must be reduced to save our environment. Doubt is never cast on whether it is too late to do anything about pollution or whether we can control it. That is just not part of the pollution narrative.

Finally, recall that when we construct a new narrative it must be done with materials already in our cognitive frameworks. Pollution meets this criterion as well.

To the extent that we reframe climate change as a narrative of pollution, we increase people's acceptance that it can be addressed through our actions. People will also readily enact a narrative that outlines concrete steps to reduce pollution. An additional benefit to a narrative that frames climate change as pollution is that many of the actions that reduce pollution are exactly the same actions scientists have been calling for in reducing the effects of climate change. If greenhouse gases are defined, discussed, and narrated as pollution, we can agree on the need to, and be inspired and motivated to, reduce greenhouse gas pollution. Language shapes our perception, and using the phrase "greenhouse gas pollution" in every place where "greenhouse gas" was formerly used will define our reality and shift our conceptualization of this pollutant.

Why does a pollution narrative resonate? Familiarity is one reason; we have enacted a pollution narrative in the past. We reduced pollution by vast amounts in the 1970s and 1980s. Reframing climate change as pollution might be considered close to a reconstruction of an existing narrative (which can be easy— even happens on autopilot) as opposed to being a new narrative construction and enactment (which is always very difficult).

■ ■ ■

This discussion about whether enactment of a narrative is completely new or is a reconstruction of an existing narrative is a great place to bring up my last narrative theory topic: narrative modes. In the previous chapter, I called on you to be reflexive about the different narratives in which you engage, and

Table 10.1 Four modes of narrative enactment

	Conscious	Unconscious
Selection (can be cued in others)	Intentional reconstruction	Autopilot
Creation	Narrative construction	Imaginative dreaming
		Unknown (not discussed)

I encouraged you to become more conscious of the narratives you go by in everyday situations. The different narrative modes are implied in the narrative enactment model, and throughout the text. Table 10.1 provides an outline of four narrative modes. One axis categorizes narrative enactment based on whether we select an existing narrative or create a new one. The other axis distinguishes our level of consciousness of the narrative we are going by.

You are already familiar with the most common mode: autopilot. When we unconsciously select and enact an existing narrative to guide us through a situation, we are going by a narrative that has us on autopilot. This mode eases most of our mundane interactions, such as buying movie tickets or shaking hands when we meet someone. We don't even realize we are going by a script. Autopilot mode has the most potential to control our actions without us being aware of that control. Enacting hidden biases can be damaging, such as an unspoken presumption that women don't make good leaders. One impact may be that we may perceive and rate a female leader's performance lower than it actually is due to our unquestioned bias.

In a work setting, this narrative puts us in danger of practicing gender discrimination.

It is beneficial to become more conscious of the narratives we go by. In intentional reconstruction mode, we are aware of the existing narrative we are selecting and why. Realizing we are going by a narrative raises our awareness of our role in various interactions. It also gives us understanding and insight into the behavior of others.

Narrative construction, the focus of this book, involves purposeful and intentional change efforts through the creation and enactment of new narratives. The narrative construction mode is exceedingly rare, but you now have the knowledge and tools to lead such transformational change efforts.

The last mode involves unconscious creation, which I have labeled "imaginative dreaming." Our focus in this book has been on purposeful and intentional change efforts, and we have not discussed this final mode. Although I believe these moments may happen, we cannot speculate about this kind of artistic subconscious imaginative mode. Accessing this mode seems more serendipitous than something that we can plan.

Your main aim is to become more conscious of the narratives you are going by. Most narratives will pressure you to act in conventional or culturally ascribed ways, but being aware of that pressure brings clarity and understanding to your everyday interactions. Being able to spot the mode others are enacting will help you decipher the actions of others. The more you apply this table, the easier it will be to predict the behavior of others and the more often you will be able to attempt change. In addition, you will have insights into the challenges your specific change efforts may present.

■ ■ ■

The jury had been deliberating for several hours on James Neely's sentence. Because this was a retrial on punishment only, the jury was determining whether he would get the death penalty. The prosecution still put on a full trial, going over the facts of the case so the jury could decide if James was deserving of death.

The judge called the jury out of the deliberation room and into the courtroom. One of the jurors sobbed uncontrollably. Makeup streamed down her cheeks. She intermittently cradled her face in her hands or lifted it to the ceiling, gulping for air as it heaved out of her chest. The judge had called for the break in deliberations so the jury could have dinner. They strolled casually into the courtroom, for the first time not entering the jury box, but standing in the area in front of the judge's bench. The jury had curiously—though not surprisingly—unconsciously assembled themselves in the middle of the courtroom in rows in the same order they usually sat in the jury box. A fellow juror patted the whimpering woman's back dutifully.

"I am going to buy you dinner now," Judge Hatch smiled like he'd tossed a coin to a collection of street urchins. "Or rather, Lincoln County is going to buy you dinner. There is a van outside. The bailiff and some deputies will go with you. Then you will return here and continue to deliberate. I remind you, you are not to discuss the case outside of the jury room."

Another burst of wailing escaped the crying juror, who muffled it by covering her face with both hands. Other jurors kept her from dropping to the floor.

"Now go on. Enjoy yourselves!" Judge Hatch said.

After the jury left, our defense team huddled. We surmised that the crying woman was being beat to hell in the deliberation room. From jury selection, we had expected her to be a possible holdout. She said she was hesitant to give the death penalty, but not against it. The prosecution wanted her dismissed based on her hesitancy. During the trial, she was the only juror who would look at James Neely.

Three hours into their deliberations, the jury had sent a note out to the judge. When that happens, the judge calls in the prosecution and defense and reads the jury note into the record. Judge Hatch waited for the court stenographer to nod that she was ready, and then read aloud the note from the jury: "In Texas, is a suicide attempt a criminal act of violence?"

The judge said he thought it may be a criminal act, but in fact, it is not. We had done all the research, but no one asked us. But no matter, the judge's lack of knowledge could not hurt us. All any judge can really do is send a note back to them saying, "Please refer to the jury instructions you have been provided," or "I cannot answer your question. Please continue to deliberate." The implicit message is that the jury has all the information they are going to get to consider. Once the trial is over, courts do not want juries bringing up new issues or inquiries. At some point, you have to draw a line, stop all the information, and send them off to make a decision.

Because of their question, we figured the jury must still be struggling on the first special issue question, the future danger question, where the jury decides if the defendant is likely to commit "criminal acts of violence" in the future. If a defendant is not going to be a danger in the future, then there is no need to kill him. The jury instructions inform the jurors that they do not even go on to the second question if at least ten jurors find the defendant will not be a future danger.

The majority of the jury must have been arguing that James is a future danger, and looking for any logic to support it. Because of Texas's absurd 10-2 rule, we also knew that they believed they had only two options: twelve jurors to vote "YES" to kill James, or at least ten to vote "NO" to spare him. Otherwise, they would have to continue to deliberate.

James was not a future danger. He had already been on death row for twenty years before the Supreme Court awarded him a retrial on punishment. During those twenty years, James had impeccable behavior on death row. He had never been involved in any altercation whatsoever, and not for lack of opportunity. During trial, we had a parade of death row guards testify to his stellar jail records and gentle demeanor. James was not a present or future danger.

I would describe James as quiet and friendly. James was in ill health, not a surprise given twenty years of solitary confinement. He was largely inept. James had not made a decision of substance in decades. He ate when he was told, did what he was told. He believed whatever he heard on talk radio. If something was funny, it was because someone else told him it was funny.

James discovered and loved Subway sandwiches, which we brought to the courthouse for lunch during his trial. Having even a small choice to make was lost on James. At Subway, you had your pick of different kinds of bread, then meat, all kinds of salad toppings, and dressings.

"Anything, man. Anything," James would say when presented with all the choices.

We literally got him everything you could put on a foot-long sandwich. He inhaled it.

"How much did that cost?" he asked.

"Five bucks."

"Is that a lot?"

On death row, James had been written up just twice in twenty years. Once he had flubbed the laundry exchange and wound up with an extra washcloth in his cell, an infraction. James still doesn't understand how he wound up with two washcloths. You give one to get one.

"Maybe two were folded up together?" he wondered.

The other infraction was that James found the end of a half-smoked marijuana joint in the cafeteria. He kept it. They found it in his cell. Both infractions had occurred more than fifteen years ago.

More recently James attempted suicide. Attempting suicide is not an infraction of any kind. The suicide attempt appeared in jail medical records. Death row inmates spend their lives in solitary confinement, a punishment used sparingly and only for short periods to discipline regular prison inmates. People become distressed in those conditions. Others go insane. One death row inmate tore out and ate his own eyeball.

James Neely was suffering from severe depression when he attempted suicide. He tied a tourniquet around his arm and sliced into his veins with a razor blade.

The jury was about to kill him for it.

I say that because I knew that the judge's nonresponse to their question about whether suicide was a criminal act would send the jury into a tailspin of frustration. Lawyers have a special name for notes sent back to the jury by the judge compelling the jury to "keep deliberating." Lawyers call it "the dynamite charge."

When the judge sends a note back to the jury that says "continue to deliberate," it usually blows up any resolve that holdouts may have. When the jury informs the judge that they are stuck, they expect some relief or guidance. They get none. Instead, they are told to just keep going. When they get the dynamite charge, jurors assume that the judge is angry and growing impatient for a verdict. They take the dynamite charge as an order from the judge to reach an agreement. When a jury notifies the judge they are stuck, judges can send as many "dynamite charges" as they like. It seldom takes more than one.

The jury had not even digested their dinner; they had been back less than twenty minutes when the bailiff went looking for the judge. They jury had reached a verdict.

James got the death penalty. Again.

Afterward I stood outside the courthouse consoling James's sister and mom. A few members of the jury came out, then the last of the court staff, followed by a few more jurors.

A few of the jurors stopped to smoke. I fretted helplessly in the knowledge that they had no idea what had just happened to them. Maybe somewhere they sensed their acquiescence. They stood an awkward distance from each other. They spoke quietly and solemnly. Small talk. They exchanged idle promises to "take care" as they parted.

The next week I was back in Lincoln County on another case, in another cell, with another killer. James Neely had already been moved back to death row, and the appeals process started all over. Before heading back to Lubbock, I called the office to see if there was anything else I could do before heading back. They asked me to meet with someone.

Right after James's trial, someone emailed our office claiming to be "one of the jurors." During high-profile trials, crazy people seem to come out of the woodwork. People offering evidence that will "prove everything" have approached me in courtroom hallways. They have grand delusions about exposing conspiracies, although they never have specifics.

One guy grabbed me to say, "The DA and government are in cahoots to kill anybody they want!" You're actually in the right ballpark, I thought, considering all of the biases in the system, but on the wrong planet.

"All the evidence is in my freezer!" he said. He also noted he was ready to take the stand if needed. I smiled politely and inched away. During the next break, a nice lady approached me to tell me that "her cat had told her everything" and that there were tremendous holes in the prosecution's case. I did not even stop walking for that one.

After trials, the public usually keeps their condemnation online in blogs or newspaper commentary, but emails to the defense team are not unheard of. When we got the email, we figured it was just another crazy person, but this emailer mentioned several convincing details and identified herself as the crying juror. Only the judge, prosecutor, and defense had been in the room when the jury broke for dinner. We wrote a nondescript single line response: "Is there something we can do for you?"

She replied that she was sorry about "what happened in the jury room." She had not been able to sleep. Could things be set right?

I felt dismissive at first. There are no such things as "second thoughts" in capital trials, river of tears be damned. Contrite jurors go to judges all the time, in all kinds of cases, confessing to horrible mistakes and massive regret, wanting to change their minds. Once you deliver a verdict, that's it. Speak then or forever hold your peace.

But I also knew our team might learn a few things. I thought about our many cases to come. More juries. What seemed most influential in their deliberations? Did they follow some process in voting? When they got stuck, what was it over? How did they reach a resolution? What did they think of this expert or that witness? I might get some ideas.

Then again, maybe she just wanted to cry again, and I would listen.

I pulled over as my cell phone battery blinked. I could get off a few more texts. Maybe. I promised that she was not doing anything wrong in asking to meet. The judge had released them from their duty. They were officially free to talk about the case. I sensed that my reassurance only heightened her anxiety. And we had all the normal complications of hammering out a meeting. We would meet at this coffee shop, and then switched it to another. This time would work better than that one, if she could get off work early, and so on. It all felt very cloak and dagger.

Any apprehension left when the juror and I recognized each other from the courtroom. I made sure my notepad was already on the table before she sat down, much less dramatic than whipping it out after the conversation begins.

"I did not want that to happen," she started. "The whole time, I just wanted to hug James and tell him that everything was going to be okay."

Well it didn't turn out okay, I wanted to say, but bit my tongue.

I asked if she remembered the two questions.

She said she would never forget them.

I asked which one they got stuck on.

"The first one." We knew that.

"What was happening in the room?" I asked.

"They kept showing me pictures of the crime scene and said, 'Do you want this to happen again?' and 'If we let him out, he'll do this again. Do you want that on your conscience?' "

"And how did you go about voting?" I asked.

"We went around the table and said our vote one at a time and talked if we wanted. One of the women wrote the votes down. If you said yes, she put a big checkmark by your name, but if you said no, she wrote down undecided. Then they would put the crime scene photos down in front of me and say things like, 'What can we do to help? How can we help you think it through?' They were trying to be consoling, but they also got frustrated every time we went around again and voted again and I said no again. The woman marking down the votes kept saying she was supposed to leave for vacation the next day."

"So what was happening when you broke for dinner?"

"I was a mess," she said.

"Were they bullying you?"

"No, it was over at that point."

"What do you mean?" I asked.

"We had just decided. And I was like, how are we supposed to eat right now?"

I pretended to sip coffee. I nodded reassuringly.

"I'm so sorry!" she started to cry. "I told that big lawyer from your side that I was the type to stand my ground. I promised him I wouldn't cave," she tried to collect herself, "but I did."

I nodded.

"I did not want this," she said. "I wanted life all along. I just didn't know how that was ever going to happen, so I folded."

I nodded.

"I just wish I could have done something, but I knew I would never convince nine of them to join me."

I nodded. I could only breathe in. I did not tell her the truth. It would have wrecked her.

Weeks later she called our office. She had done some research. There was no need to protect her now. She knew all about the 10-2 rule.

"That's how it really works?" she fumed. The jurors had imagined a mistrial. If she had known the truth, she swore James would have gotten life—or they would still be in that room.

She went to visit James on death row.

She started taking legal classes and applied to law school.

She sends all her grades to James.

Conclusion

L et us revisit the model of narrative change one more time (see figure). I think it is comprehensive and widely applicable. I tell my students to tape the change model on a wall where they will see it every day. It explains all of our actions and the actions of others, and it holds the keys to changing them. Even if we do not have big changes in mind, using the model enables us to question how we think and act, and in doing so, we can create new ways of acting and thinking for ourselves.

We must first become aware of how narratives pressure us to act, behave, and see things in particular ways. Very often, we simply adopt narratives while being socialized into our culture. Narratives are useful. They help us navigate situations and guide us through interactions, but at the same time, they control the actions we take. Most often, we simply go by the same old narratives in a routinized fashion and continually reconstruct them. In doing this, narratives become more institutionalized and more powerful. If we are not conscious of the narratives we follow, if we are on autopilot, we do not have a chance at change.

In leading change, we attempt to create new narratives and enact them. After becoming aware of and deconstructing any controlling narratives, we can create new ones. Deconstructing

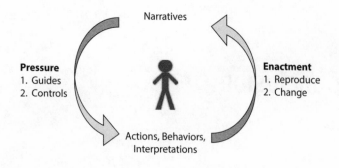

Figure Con.1 The narrative change model revisited

Source: Figure by the author

existing narratives loosens their control over us and gives us more confidence to rely on and "go by" our own narratives. The old narratives are just as made up as our new narrative, so why not go by a narrative that brings our designs of the future into reality?

Once we create our own narrative and commit to going by it to guide our actions, we have a chance to enact the narrative and act its plot into being. We must perform our vision into concrete existence.

I believe the narrative change model works for almost any type of change. It can be used at the team level, but also across an organization or to organize a community. It can be used for large-scale, transformational change and to launch massive social change. A few people with a good narrative can change the world.

I agree with my fellow ethnographer Margaret Mead, who said, "Never doubt that a small group of thoughtful, committed citizens can change the world. Indeed, it's the only thing that ever has." Any future you can describe in a narrative is possible.

I have used the narrative change model in several contexts beyond changing the way the death penalty works in Texas.

I used it to help develop a new brand narrative for Burt's Bees, a tremendously fun company that wanted to leave much of their unique identity intact while expanding their brand into new markets. They created a narrative in which both were possible.

My colleagues and I helped Unilever's top marketing and management team explore ways to live and enact their corporate values. Unilever has strongly held values around sustainability. Developing a narrative enabled them to envision new ways to approach their work while considering that sustainability value. Some of the leaders at Unilever were interested in developing personal leadership narratives, so I shared my own personal leadership narrative: Can you do it when it's hard? I challenged Unilever executives to pursue their values even if it was hard to do so. We discussed what that might mean for their work and tried to identify times when enacting their values may be challenging. There were powerful reactions. It really resonated with them because committing to be sustainable is hard. They also knew that pursuing their values was probably most important when it was hard to do so.

In New Zealand, I directed a narrative workshop to help a government social services group better understand their own processes and how to better serve their community. We developed a narrative that represented their current work as well as envisioned a new narrative. It helped to overcome the challenge of being pressured to stick to current narratives. It made explicit the narratives the team would have to resist while they enacted their new narrative. It helped the entire organization develop a shared understanding about what they were doing, their impact, and how they might do it better. The result was a massive amount of insight and self-understanding. We also learned for the first time how important a role some of their stakeholders played in their work.

This team served at-risk or troubled youth. They realized the existing narrative they were all going by might be titled "keep them out of trouble." If any of the youths got in trouble with the law, or had truancy or disciplinary problems in school, there were curfews and social worker check-ins and lots of control mechanisms to keep the kids out of trouble.

The new narrative they created told a story of success for their clients, not control. They went from a " keep them out of trouble " narrative to a "launch them into success" narrative. Kids meeting all their goals "got" to participate in additional training and skill-building programs. The narrative focused on goal achievement and specific accomplishments rather than just staying out of trouble. Parents, school staff, social workers, and the clients all became active participants in growth rather than control. The narrative they created completely changed their orientation toward their work and was more rewarding and motivating for the social workers. I thought job satisfaction would improve along with having much more meaningful outcomes for all stakeholders.

At the individual level, I have run many leadership narrative workshops with my undergraduate students and executives. Everyone found that the model gave them personal insight into their own behavior, and many have reported positive results. At the very least, developing a personal leadership narrative has provided both purpose and direction as well as a list of concrete actions they can take to pursue their goals and ambitions.

I recently conducted a narrative workshop for Clorox, the consumer products company, to create narratives to enact their strategic vision. I met with the top executives at Clorox, and we spent a lot of time creating strategic narratives. This group was so intelligent, creative, and open to the entire process that they decided to perform their new narratives in skits as a way to communicate them! But even before the powerful performances, practicing how the narratives might look and feel deepened the development of the narratives. For example, like many consumer product companies, they plan to become more and more consumer-oriented. I think a lot of companies share this goal, but few can tell you exactly what it looks like. Clorox created a narrative that consisted of several actionable plots that showed how this closer interaction would happen. The consumer, along with Clorox, was a central character in the narrative. Creating this particular narrative not only made their strategy more concrete and performative but provided Clorox with a ton of empathy for the consumer experience. They had taken on the role of the consumer in creating their corporate narrative. It really was all about the consumer. They envisioned and acted out how they wished the consumer would interact with Clorox brands and provided ideas for how they could behave to make those interactions and experiences lead to what Clorox called "irrational loyalty." They wanted consumers to go out of their way, even beyond reason, to buy and use Clorox products. I won't share their specific scripts for building and maintaining brand loyalty, but don't be surprised if you see more and more Clorox brands becoming what the marketing industry refers to as "beloved brands."

Clorox also created some internally focused operational narratives, redefining the way they wanted to work. One brilliant insight was that they didn't really need more and more data. What they needed was faster and more responsive decision-making. Executives created a narrative that will improve their responsiveness. I liked this narrative because the increased reliance on data analytics so common today has sparked a trend to overly focus on gathering and analyzing all the big data available. Just because we can do something doesn't mean we should do it. It may not be the best use of resources and time.

Analyzing everything can be costly, and the return is questionable. Companies know a lot about their consumers, and the level of detail becomes more surprising every day. But getting more and more data for the sake of having more data, just because it is available, is akin to a baseball team thinking that buying more bats will get them more hits. You do need a bat to get a hit, but more bats do not equate to more hits. The executives at Clorox are very smart about optimal and focused data analysis—they wanted more hits, not more bats. If the data or analysis did not help them make faster decisions or improve the consumer experience, Clorox decided they would eliminate it. Clorox laid out a plan to swim through the data that is drowning the rest of us.

Those are just a few examples of contexts where narrative change has been applied. Of course, I would love to hear from you about other uses for the narrative change model. I hope to learn a lot from your own attempts to apply the model.

■ ■ ■

Uber still faces a rough road. They had all the aspiration they needed, but in the end Uber lacked a narrative. The IPO was a flop. Stock price fell around 20 percent in the first two days of trading. The new CEO saw a $100 million bonus evaporate. Six months after the IPO, Uber's value is down a third and still declining.

Uber's reputation for mistreating employees remains largely unchanged. Drivers have organized strikes to protest the pay structure, poor working conditions, and a lack of transparency of corporate operations.

Uber made the mistake I have cautioned against most. One of the biggest challenges to narrative change is resisting the existing narratives while simultaneously enacting a new narrative.

You cannot just say "we are going to do things in a new way" without addressing the old way of doing things. Ignoring all the damaging existing narratives has perhaps been the main downfall of Uber's transformational change effort. The other mistake Uber made was thinking that the only changes they needed to make were internal. You must include all of your stakeholders when creating your new narrative. Your customers need to be part of your story.

Uber needs to become more inclusive, and a co-created narrative can achieve that. As long as there is a lack of transparency, a lack of trust will be impossible to overcome. There are walls all around Uber. There is no easy way for customers to reach live customer service. That is an unintentional narrative that Uber has created. Customers fret when they have a customer service issue, knowing there is no way to reach anyone. A lonely, isolated customer experience is the result. Drivers also feel a separation from Uber. Drivers do not see a role for them in the company's overall goal—because they don't have one. Alternatively, drivers could be coparticipants in constructing a new narrative and enacting Uber's future; a narrative with a clear role for drivers and a strategy for achieving multiple goals.

If Uber does not construct a new narrative for themselves, others will, and they may not like the ending.

■ ■ ■

My involvement with the death penalty was deeply satisfying for me, but other opportunities have come about as a result. I won an Embrey Human Rights Fellowship at Southern Methodist University in recognition of my work fighting the death penalty. SMU is one of the few universities in the country that has a human rights program. Columbia University is another, and I hope more universities will add this and other types of activism as programs of study. At Texas Tech, I was able to offer an elective MBA course titled Human Rights and the Corporation that was transformative for students. I think a focus on human rights will distinguish them as they enter, and one day lead, corporations.

As part of that human rights fellowship, I studied the Holocaust and toured almost every extermination camp in Poland. That somber experience gave me new insights into how made up narratives can be used to do great harm. I think this risk remains for my change model. Understanding how the narrative change model works may help us keep others from enacting evil narratives. We can commit to deconstructing harmful narratives.

That trip also came at a good time for me, because I had so long felt tormented by the up-close street fight against the death penalty. I am not comparing or relating my experience to anyone else's suffering. Mine amounts to nothing. All of the Human Rights Fellows read and discussed Holocaust survivor Viktor Frankl's book, *Man's Search for Meaning*. Frankl had some inspiring, yet counterintuitive, thoughts on suffering. He encourages us not to wallow in suffering, nor to let it defeat us. Instead he advises that we search for meaning in it. Yes, learn from suffering. Frankl achieved this during this own suffering in the horrific conditions he faced during the Holocaust. He said, if we find ourselves in times of great suffering, we should pray that we are worthy of it. He did not mean that anyone deserves to suffer but that we can hope to be deserving of the lessons that suffering brings—that the pain is not lost on us. That we grow. That we find meaning in our suffering.

The narrative change model came directly out of my death penalty defense work. The model helped us change the death penalty, and it helped me make sense of what we were doing. It gave me a purpose. I do not regret that experience, even the painful parts. I am so grateful for it. I hope I am deserving of its lessons.

■ ■ ■

There were some fun and surreal moments on my journey too. I went to Hollywood and met Steven Spielberg. Along with this book, I had a proposal for a narrative nonfiction book about the death penalty defense team. It was a story about the origins of the team, the people who do death penalty work, what motivates them to keep going against all odds, and how they wrestle in torment to save people that society wants to kill. I tried to make that book read like a John Grisham thriller. I wanted readers to encounter the death penalty world as I had—an outsider-cum-insider—and discover the inner workings of the system alongside me, sharing in all my bafflement and anger but also in the pride I have for the people who do this thankless work. The members of the death penalty defense team have been heroes of mine since our first meeting. I really wanted to tell their story and show why they do what they do.

I met an agent/producer who eventually became my agent. Kathy Carter came to the death penalty defense team as an executive producer, inquiring about doing some sort of reality TV show on the team. Kathy had twenty years of experience as an agent and a producer. Michael and I met with her in Dallas right around the time we were getting a reputation for changing the way the death penalty works. Kathy had a lawyer friend who said she should look into our story. Kathy pitched following the team around with cameras. Reality TV shows about live police investigations were very popular at that time. People loved watching cops solve crimes in one-hour episodes. She thought a documentary from the defense side might garner the same kind of interest.

None of it was possible given client-attorney privilege. Also, our clients were all charged with the death penalty and still awaiting trial. It was a horrible idea, and from our perspective it would be harmful to have any of it filmed. It was probably a violation of the law, if not just bad for the defense. Kathy took the news well and shrugged.

"Okay. That's what I came to find out."

Kathy kept in touch with me over the years. After my research engagement ended, she sent my book proposal to her former colleagues at the William Morris Agency. The agency is famous for representing top Hollywood talent, but they also had a literary division. Kathy had worked on the talent agency side for years, and she called in a favor to have someone in the literary division look at my proposal and see if anyone wanted to represent it to publishers.

Kathy texted me three days later: How soon can you be in L.A.? I was boarding a plane for LAX when she clarified that no one was interested in publishing the book.

"They hated it," she told me. No one wants to read a book about people who help killers. However, some people wanted to talk about buying the screen rights to my life. "Once word got out that some bigger players wanted to meet, it snowballed, and all kinds of requests to meet came in," Kathy explained. "It was like a feeding frenzy. But don't worry, we're only meeting with the best."

"Wait," I asked, "they don't like the book, but they want to buy the screen rights for the book they hate?"

"You got it."

"So if someone buys the screen rights, can I still write the book?"

"Knock yourself out."

Even on the way to the first meeting, I was apprehensive. I had no experience with anything like this, and images of unscrupulous Hollywood had been flooding my mind for two days. I was certain that slick swindlers would con me out of my life savings, little as it was. Hollywood had already hurt my feelings by hating my book. Now Hollywood was sure to chew me up and spit me out before I knew what happened.

Our first meeting was with Amblin Entertainment, Steven Spielberg's production company. We were supposed to discuss a show about my unintended involvement and the people who do death penalty defense work. Each episode would be character driven, following members of the defense team through death penalty cases but also at home each night to see how the work affected their lives. I liked this framing because it had the most similarities with the book I was writing.

We drove to Universal Pictures studio, just past the main Universal theme park entrance to a secured entryway. We checked in at a guard booth and drove into the studios alongside the Los Angeles River. To our right were all the studio buildings, and beyond them, a wall that separated the studios from the theme park.

It started to feel like this might not be a hoax after all. My mouth must have been gaping.

"Have you ever been to the theme park?" Kathy saw me looking at it. "It's actually fun."

"No, but I can't believe they keep the actual stars just behind the theme park."

Steven Spielberg had a separate compound within the larger studio property deep into the lots. We checked into his guard booth and were waived through. The attendant recognized Kathy. The main building reminded me of a Santa Fe hacienda, a large adobe house with an enclosed courtyard. Kathy and I waited in the reception area while the guards ticked off things on lists and picked up the phone to tell someone we had arrived. Someone would come to collect us from another building in the complex. The reception area was decorated with Academy Awards in glass-enclosed cases. There were various pieces of filmmaking memorabilia, including the old movie camera used to film *Jaws*.

As I was milling around the lobby, I saw a golf cart pull up at the front door. A guy with a beard in a bulky cable knit cardigan with a massive rolled collar got out and came toward the door. It can't be, I thought, but it was. Steven Spielberg opened the door, walked past the reception desk, and gave me a friendly nod. My mind raced with awe and the urgency to say something sincere and brilliant. I managed to turn and face him directly as he approached. "Hi there" was all I could manage, but I assure you, I was very cool and calm, just like it was no big deal.

"Hello, how are you?" he gave me a nod as he passed and opened the opposite door. He stepped into the courtyard interior and went up some stairs on his left. I stutter stepped toward the door, hoping to catch it before it closed, to yell up after him: "I am here to meet with some of your people!" The door swung shut before I could embarrass myself.

I dragged my chin across the floor to find my agent sunk into a plush leather couch, her face down and thumbs hammering away on her phone, as she had been doing since we arrived.

"That was Steve Spielberg!" I whisper-shouted at her. "What are the chances?"

"Pretty good," she did not look up, "we *are* in his office."

For our next meeting, I had to take an Uber across town to Sony Picture studios. Kathy had another meeting but would meet me there. The meeting at Sony Pictures was with the people who ran all the CSI shows. Their idea was further afield from my book, and much further afield from reality. They wondered if someone could be exonerated from death row in each episode. My character would be akin to some kind of mastermind FBI profiler, but for the defense. We would use all kinds of CSI techniques, and my wits, apparently, to prove some convicted killer was innocent.

My Uber had to drop me off at the end of a long entry drive to Sony Pictures. I would have to walk the rest of the way. "This is as far as I can go," my driver apologized and nodded toward a huge guardhouse at the end of a long drive.

I got out and began to walk down the drive; there was no sidewalk. Limousines and Bentley's careened around me; as they approached the guardhouse, a crossbeam barricading the entrance raised and lowered to let them pass. Through the glass I saw the silhouettes of five big guards wearing hats that made them look like policemen. The shadows all turned toward me. They must not get many walkers. They probably had me pegged as some star-struck lunatic. I imagined them preparing to get rid of me, trying nicely at first.

One of the guards stepped into the lane for approaching cars when I was still ten yards away, adding himself to the barricade. "Can I help you?" he asked.

"I have an appointment," I said. We were now in what appeared to be a standoff. He positioned himself so I could not make a run past the barricade, and another guard in the doorway hit a button as a limo approached. I had to step toward the guardhouse to avoid being run over. I stepped backward into the driveway once the car passed, playing Frogger with approaching traffic. A pause in traffic allowed the guard to stick his hand out impatiently, "Gimmie your ID."

"It's Hans Hansen." I said. He didn't care what I said, he cared what my ID said. He snapped it from my fumbling hands, more as a favor really. The four other guards had turned around to witness our exchange, their faces chiseled in an amazing lack of expression.

The guard with my ID glanced down at my feet before he
stepped back into the guardhouse. Stay right there, it meant.

He put my ID atop a keyboard as he typed away. He clicked
the mouse and peered at the screen and then back at my ID and
then finally to me, then the screen again. He turned to the other
guards, "He's actually on the list."

Their faces finally cracked. They exchanged, "well, who
woulda thunk it?" smirks. Maybe they had bets.

"Step in here, young man!" the guard bellowed and slapped
me on the back. "Get in here in the air conditioning."

I told him about being summoned to Hollywood the day
before yesterday and that I was supposed to be having a meeting
about selling the rights to my life.

"Welcome to Hollywood!" he beamed. "Do you know where
you're going?" he asked.

"No," I said. "How do I look?" I presented myself before him
like he was a full-length mirror.

"Super!" He handed me back my ID and checked the com-
puter again. "Okay, let's see here. Sorry, I've never given anyone walking instructions. Okay, you are going to go all the way
down to that big yellow building. See it way down there? You're
going to take a right at that street, then keep straight until you
see the car from Ghostbusters. Do you know that car? The sta-
tion wagon with all the junk on it?"

"I think so."

"You can't miss it. It's parked in front of the building you
need." He gave me a much-needed push out the door to get my
feet moving.

Both of my Hollywood meetings had been scheduled for
thirty minutes. Both lasted two hours. Kathy would only go as
far as saying that it wasn't discouraging. We even sketched out

some story lines and episodes with the executives so they would have something concrete to think about, they said.

"But people don't get exonerated from death row every week," I told them.

"They will on the show," one of the executives said.

"Have you ever had any romantic interest with a sexy DA that wanted to kill your client?" another asked.

"Ummm . . . no," I said. That was even more implausible than me being some sort of mastermind.

"You will on the show," the executive said dryly.

Kathy had explained all this to me. "If they buy the rights to your story, it's theirs. They can do anything they want with it."

"But none of their ideas ever really happen," I said, already knowing that it could not have mattered less.

"They will put together whatever they think will sell. But don't worry, even if they do buy the screen rights, the chances are very low that you'll ever see an episode." When studios buy screen rights, most of the time they let them sit and never do anything with them. "We would only option the rights for five years to make sure we can have them back if they don't ever produce a show," Kathy said.

"So I could get my life back?" I asked.

"Yes," she said, "if they aren't interested in it. When they buy screen rights, they only make a pilot for about one in twenty of them, and that's just one pilot. Then, out of all the pilots they shoot, maybe one in twenty of those is selected for a full season, then they make six to fifteen episodes. Out of all the shows produced with a full first season, one in twenty of those gets picked for a second season, and even fewer get a third season, and so on."

"But if we sell, we don't have to do anything else, right?"

"Well," she continued, "you have to hope it makes it, because we will get a cut of any profits in perpetuity."

"And are profits likely?" I asked.

"No. Not until you get to season three or so. On the other hand, if you get lucky enough to have a show that goes five seasons or more, it gets big. You won't be a professor anymore."

"But I like being a professor."

"You would probably need to move here. If you pass five seasons, there will be spinoffs and other opportunities will start to come to you."

"But couldn't I still be a professor?" I asked.

"Knock yourself out," she sighed.

■ ■ ■

Well, I'm still just a professor. My Hollywood adventure lasted one day. It turned out that people wanted a TV show about helping killers as much as they wanted a book about it.

On a brighter note, I am happy to report that I did get tenure, so I will be a professor for quite a while if I like. The tenure process was precarious, but it went better than I hoped. I am told the vote at the college level was unanimous, the first unanimous vote in some time. The university and Board of Regents approved my tenure without reservation and made everything official.

Academic principles say tenure supposedly frees us to do whatever kind of research we want, but I do not think my priorities will change. I was not waiting for tenure to pursue my convictions, and I was ready for what they might cost me.

Every field has norms about how long you have to wait to be able to do certain things, and rules about who has "permission" to engage in various pursuits. I suggest that you try to ignore those rules and focus on making a contribution. Maybe it is doing what you love, or doing what you are good at—both if you are lucky.

I am also grateful for my colleagues. I know how fortunate I am to be at such a great university in Texas Tech. Admittedly, the department has carried me. We are judged, individually and as a department, for better or worse, on the number of academic articles we publish in peer-reviewed journals. My colleagues churn out plenty of journal articles. Compared to them, I do not pull my weight for the team. Being able to pursue both my passions and my unconventional research agenda is rare. I have great colleagues and tremendous freedom.

Many of you may be in jobs that you find too constraining. I know college graduates cross the stage with high aspirations and all sorts of vigor. Then they get into a job, and it turns into a grind, and eventually grinds on them. Many of us end up compromising on our dreams.

Do not give up. Focus on your own contribution, no matter what value others place on it. Try to measure yourself by how much you give, not how much you get. And do not compare the two. I suppose I will always struggle to overcome various fears and self-centeredness, but deep down I like to think I would rather make a difference than make a dollar. From what I have seen, the people who do the former don't have to worry about the latter.

Our little ragtag team from Texas changed the world. The people doing death penalty defense work are all heroes, but each still has defects of character. They are all so human. When we formed, some had sworn off the death penalty, others had been broken, and a few had nowhere else to go. Still, we came together and formulated a vision, constructed a narrative, and managed to enact it. It was not always easy, and our own culture was difficult to sustain as we grew. Our performance skyrocketed against miraculous odds, and then it slowly leveled off. As for the impact on the death penalty over all, I am sure there is no going back to the old way of doing things. Our new narratives have become institutionalized. I do not know if we are in the last days of the death penalty, but certainly fewer and fewer people will be sentenced to die.

Whatever your pursuits, I hope you find the narrative change model useful. If you are leading change in any organization, it can provide a lot of guidance. If you just want to develop a personal leadership narrative, make one that resonates with you and drives you toward great accomplishments.

Narratives are all we have to go by. We might as well create great ones. My hope for you is that knowing how to narrate change will help you transform the world, or just yourself. Both are valuable, and there may not be as much difference between the two as you think.

Notes

Introduction

1. Most popular models of change reflect Lewin's (1948) model, which roughly describes unfreezing, changing, and refreezing as three steps to change.
2. See Czarniawska (1997b) for the basic elements of narratives.
3. For more on narrative as a mode of thinking and organizing our interpretive world, see Bruner (1986).
4. Karl Weick (1995) describes sense making and how we create accounts of our experiences in an attempt to integrate events into a coherent narrative.
5. Czarniawska (1997a, 1997b) describes narrative as a primary source of organizing.
6. See Bass (1985) and Collins and Porras (1996) for more on the importance of building a vision as an essential part of an organizational change process.
7. Bruner (1990) describes this function of the narrative mode of thinking.
8. Institutional theory has described these pressures to conform to norms. Some foundational thoughts can be found in DiMaggio and Powell (1983), Meyer and Rowan (1977), and Zucker (1977).
9. DiMaggio and Powell (1983) talk about how this "taken-for-grantedness" results in unconscious decisions rather than deliberate or strategic decisions.
10. Holm (1995) and Seo and Creed (2002) describe this challenge to change the very structures that control us—a change from inside the system—the paradox of embeddedness.

1. No Place to Hide

1. Peters and Waterman (1982) looked for what distinguished top companies and found organizational culture to be a significant differentiator. Theories regarding organizational culture became a top pursuit in research and practice.
2. Van Maanen (1975) was influential in bringing ethnography into organizational studies. He conducted ethnographic research by going through police training.

2. Talking Narratives

1. Turner (2011).
2. See the *New York Times* article by Greenhouse (2002) for details on this and other examples.

3. How the Change Model Emerged

1. See Boje (2001) for more on organizational narratives.
2. Anthony Giddens (1984) created structuration theory.
3. The narrative way of knowing was contrasted with more rational models and is advanced by Bruner (1986), Polkinghorne (1988), and Czarniawska (1997a).

4. Applying the Model

1. Black (1976) presents a sociological perspective on inequality in the justice system.
2. For more research and statistics on race and death penalty sentencing, see The Death Penalty Information Center (https://deathpenaltyinfo.org/policy-issues/race/ways-that-race-can-affect-death-sentencing).

5. The Narrative Stranglehold

1. In addition to the institutional theorists mentioned in the text, see Scott (2013).
2. See Garfinkel (1967).

3. Stouten, Rousseau, and De Cremer (2018) reviewed the top change models, and none of these models addressed the current way of doing things as being a severe impediment to change. Only Lewin (1948) emphasized the need to question existing views as part of change.
4. William J. Bowers (1994) runs the Capital Jury Research Project, which researches how people who serve as jurors on capital cases make the life or death sentencing decision.

6. Enacting New Narratives

1. Bowers (1994).
2. David Boje (2001) calls these not yet enacted narratives "antenarratives" to signify that they are prenarratives and also somewhat of a bet on the future.
3. For more on enacted narratives as a way to understand social life, see MacIntyre (1981).
4. See Lévi-Strauss and Layton (1963).
5. See Conley (2016) and Conley-Riner (2017) for more on how language and narrative play a role in capital jury sentencing decisions, as well as their deference to the judge in making this decision.

7. Narrative Selection vs. Narrative Construction

1. See Charles Sanders Peirce (1931), a founder of pragmatism, for more on abduction and abductive thinking.
2. This story comes from Karl Weick (1993) as an example of the sense-making process. I believe abduction can reestablish sense making when it collapses.

8. Narratives as a Way to Organize

1. *Defending the Damned* by Kevin Davis (2008) details the stories of capital crime defense attorneys who are routinely asked, "How can you defend these people?" It was cathartic for me.

References

Bass, B. M. (1985). *Leadership and Performance Beyond Expectations.* New York: Collier Macmillan.

Black, D. (1976). *The Behavior of the Law.* Bingley, UK: Emerald Group.

Boje, D. M. (2001). *Narrative Methods for Organizational & Communication Research.* Newbury Park, Calif.: Sage.

Bowers, W. J. (1994). The capital jury project: Rationale, design, and preview of early findings. *Indiana Law Journal, 70,* 1043–1102.

Bruner, J. S. (1986). *Actual Minds, Possible Worlds.* Cambridge, Mass.: Harvard University Press.

———. (1990). *Acts of Meaning.* Cambridge, Mass.: Harvard University Press.

Collins, J. C., & Porras, J. I. (1996). Building your company's vision. *Harvard Business Review, 74*(5), 65.

Conley, R. (2016). *Confronting the Death Penalty: How Language Influences Jurors in Capital Cases.* Cambridge, UK: Oxford University Press.

Conley-Riner, R. (2017). Discourses of death: The influence of language on capital jurors' decisions. *Journal of Criminal Justice & Law 1*(1), 43–56.

Czarniawska, B. (1997a). *Narrating the Organization: Dramas of Institutional Identity.* Chicago, Ill.: University of Chicago Press.

———, ed. (1997b). *A Narrative Approach to Organization Studies.* Newbury Park, Calif.: Sage.

Davis, K. (2008). *Defending the Damned: Inside a Dark Corner of the Criminal Justice System.* New York: Atria Books.

DiMaggio, P. J., & Powell, W. W. (1983). The iron cage revisited: Institutional isomorphism and collective rationality in organizational fields. *American Sociological Review, 48*(2), 147–160.

Garfinkel, H. (1967). *Studies in Ethnomethodology.* Upper Saddle River, N.J.: Prentice-Hall.

Giddens, A. (1984). *The Constitution of Society: Outline of the Theory of Structuration.* Berkeley, Calif.: University of California Press.

Greenhouse, L. (2002, June 4). Inmate whose lawyer slept gets new trial. *New York Times*, p. A16.

Holm, P. (1995). The dynamics of institutionalization: Transformation processes in Norwegian fisheries. *Administrative Science Quarterly, 40,* 398–422.

Lévi-Strauss, C., & Layton, M. (1963). *Structural Anthropology.* New York: Basic Books.

Lewin, K. (1948). *Resolving Social Conflicts: Selected Papers on Group Dynamics.* New York: Harper.

MacIntyre, A. (1981). *After Virtue.* London: Duckworth.

Meyer & Rowan (1977). Institutionalized organizations: Formal structure as myth and ceremony. *American journal of sociology, 83*(2), 340–363.

Peirce, C. S. (1931). *Collected Papers of Charles Sanders Peirce.* Cambridge, Mass.: Harvard University Press.

Peters, T. J., & Waterman, R. H. (1982). *In Search of Excellence: Lessons from America's Best-Run Companies.* New York: Harper & Row.

Polkinghorne, D. E. (1988). *Narrative Knowing and the Human Sciences.* Albany, N.Y.: State University of New York Press.

Scott, W. R. (2013). *Institutions and Organizations: Ideas, Interests, and Identities,* 4th ed. Newbury Park, Calif.: Sage.

Seo, M. G., & Creed, W. D. (2002). Institutional contradictions, praxis, and institutional change: A dialectical perspective. *Academy of Management Review, 27*(2), 222–247.

Stouten, J., Rousseau, D. M., & De Cremer, D. (2018). Successful organizational change: Integrating the management practice and scholarly literatures. *Academy of Management Annals, 12*(2), 752–788.

Turner, A. 2011. Hate crime killer executed. *Houston Chronicle*, September 22, 2011. https://www.chron.com/news/houston-texas/article/Hate-crime-killer -executed-2182684.php

Van Maanen, J. (1975). Police socialization: A longitudinal examination of job attitudes in an urban police department. *Administrative Science Quarterly, 20,* 207–228.

Weick, K. E. (1993). The collapse of sensemaking in organizations: The Mann Gulch disaster. *Administrative Science Quarterly, 38*(4), 628–652.

———. (1995). *Sensemaking in Organizations.* Newbury Park, Calif.: Sage.

Zucker, L. G. (1977). The role of institutionalization in cultural persistence. *American sociological review, 42*(5), 726–743.

Index

Page numbers in *italics* refer to illustrations or tables.

abductive thinking, 114, 115, 116–117, 120, 129, 193n1

abuse, 87–88

academic journals, 25, 188

actionability, 123

actions, 4, 52–53, 119, 131–132; categorizing, 122–123; change loops within, *105*, 106; climate change, 159, 160, 161; as guided, 5–6, 7, 48, 56, 162, 173; reconstructive loops within, 77, *78*, 146, 161; as wrong, 89

addiction, alcohol, 50, 54, 92, 107–108, 127, 147–148

aggravating circumstances, 59, 61

alcohol addiction, 50, 54, 92, 107–108, 127, 147–148

Amblin Entertainment, 183

amendments, of U.S. Constitution, 58, 95–96

American Bar Association, 29, 32

analogies, for jury deliberations, 101–102, 103, 104

analytics, data, 177–178

anecdotal evidence, 23, 135

anomalies, 116

anthropologists, 53, 106

appeals process, 64

appellate courts, 29, 64–65, 68–69, 134

appellate procedure, 68, 69

Archaeopteryx fossil, 116

Arkansas, 18

armchair psychology, 99

articles, in academic journals, 25, 188

aspirations, 152–153, 156–157, 158, 178

assumptions, 132, 146, 151, 160; cultural, 56; "do the right thing" narrative, 156; rational, 84; underlying, 129

attorneys, 28–29, 30–31, 65–67; Graham, 96; Kape, 124–125; Toby, 22, 95–96, 97. *See also* defense attorneys; district attorney

autopilot, 129, 161, 162, 173

awards, death penalty defense team winning, 135

backstabbing, 89, 144
"bad boy" behavior, 73–74
bailiffs, 139, 140, 141
Barney's (department store), 154–155
Behavior of Law, The (Black), 59–60
behaviors, 86, 118; "bad boy,"
    73–74; cultural, 55; norms of, 52;
    reconstructive, 78
benefits, of construction process, 130
Best Public Safety Office (award), 135
bias, 62, 64, 162–163, 168
bifurcated trial, 58
bird droppings, 3–4
Black, Donald, 59–60
Block, Michael, 24–25, 27, 28, 31–32,
    33–34, 39–41
blood, 21
blueprint, logic, 4
Boje, David, 44–45, 192n1, 193n2
book proposal, death penalty
    defense team, 181, 182–183
bottom line, 148
Bowers, William J., 193n4
"the boy who cried wolf," 52
breakups, 111, 112
Brewer, Lawrence, 27–28
"bro culture," at Uber, 73–74, 90
building: teams, 24, 43, 130–132,
    175–176; trust, 85–86, 88, 129, 132
Burt's Bees, 175
business schools, 13, 25, 91–92, 138
Byrd, James, Jr., 27–28

Calvert, Larry, 107, 140–141
"Can you do it when it's hard?"
    narrative, 157, 175

Capital Case Bench Book, 29
Capital Jury Research Project, 83,
    104, 193n4
"Capital Murder Charges" headline,
    136
capital-qualified list, 30–31
Carter, Kathy, 181–182, 183, 184,
    186–187
cases, death penalty, 28–30, 32–33,
    67, 101
categorizing actions, 122–123
challenges, 123–124, 153
changes: action loops of, 105, 106;
    climate, 159, 160, 161; narrative
    model of, 51, 71, 145, 151, 173, 174,
    175. See also specific topics
character defects, 85, 150, 189
character generating (storytelling),
    121–122
circumstances: aggravating, 59, 61;
    mitigating, 88, 140
client-attorney privilege, 182
climate change, 159, 160, 161
climate change denial, 159, 160
Clorox, 176–178
co (with), 93
Code of Criminal Procedure, Texas,
    68
cognitive frameworks, 49, 51, 77, 81,
    98, 117; control by, 151; DA, 133;
    pollution, 161
commitment, 103
communications, 111–112
community, 121
compassion, 93
compromise, 189

concepts, 1, 6, 129; framework for, 160; new, 99, 100, 114–115

confinement, solitary, 167

"conflictioneering" narrative, 138

Conley-Riner, Robin, 106–107, 139, 141, 193n5

Constitution, U.S., 66–67, 138; constitutional rights, 31; Eighth Amendment, 58, 95–96

construction process, benefits of, 130

consumers, 148, 153, 177–178, 179

control, 36, 37, 39, 151

convictions, 10, 92, 152, 153–154, 156–157

coordinated team, 130–131

corporate: culture, 9, 26, 44; values, 175

costs, 54, 133–134

court appointment lists, 30

Court of Criminal Appeals, 97

court records, 63–64, 65, 69, 98

courtroom objections, 63

courts: appellate, 29, 64–65, 68–69, 134; appointment lists, 30; records, 63–64, 65, 69, 98; Supreme Court, 58, 60, 61, 70, 96, 97–98

creation, 162; pattern, 115; selection vs., 109

creative discussion, 15

creativity, 119–120

crime scene investigation (CSI), 184–185

Criminal Defense Lawyers Association, Texas, 28, 31

critical thinking, 114

CSI (crime scene investigation), 184–185

culture, 3–4, 38, 51; assumptions of, 56; behaviors of, 55; "bro culture," 73–74, 90; corporate, 9, 26, 44; of defense attorneys, 104–105; new, 8; norms, 102; organizational, 13–14, 46–47, 50, 192n1; positive, 40; pressures, 163; strong, 132; values, 142–143

customers, 148, 153, 177–178, 179

Czarniawska, B., 191n2, 191n5

DA. See district attorney

data analytics, 177–178

Davis, Kevin, 193n1

death penalty, 8, 40, 92, 127; cases, 28–30, 32–33, 67, 101; defense attorneys, 10, 28, 97; factors for, 27, 59; history of, 58; impact on, 190; race and, 60–61; for Rose, 19; as unconstitutional, 96, 97; waiving, 136

death penalty defense team, 12–13, 14, 15–16, 28, 189; awards won by, 135; book proposal, 181, 182–183; emails to, 168–169; guidelines for, 32–33

Death Penalty Information Center, 192n2

death sentences, in Texas, 16, 17, 58, 79–80, 83

deconstruction, 114, 151, 152, 153, 173–174

deduction, 114

defects, character, 85, 150, 189

Defending the Damned (Davis), 193n1

defense attorneys, 66–67, 82, 100, 108; culture of, 104–105; death penalty, 10, 28, 97; seminar for, 137

defense motions, 94

defense team, death penalty, 12–13, 14, 15–16, 28, 189; awards won by, 135; book proposal, 181, 182–183; emails to, 168–169; guidelines for, 32–33

deference, 66–67, 136

deliberations, jury, 100, 139–140, 164–165, 167–168; analogies for, 101–102, 103–104; on Neely, 167–168, 170–171

denial, climate change, 159, 160

DiMaggio, P. J., 191nn8–9

district attorney (DA), 16, 32, 124, 187; cognitive frameworks, 133; as elected official, 134; jurors coached by, 94–95; Kape calls with, 136–137

distrust, 84–85, 118, 179

"do the right thing" narrative, 154–155, 158; assumptions of, 156; Uber, 143–144

drunk dreams, 92

"the dynamite charge," 167

Ecole Supérieure de Commerce, 45

education, of jurors, 99–100

Eighth Amendment, U.S. Constitution, 58, 95–96

elected official, DA as, 134

emails, to death penalty defense team, 168–169

Embrey Human Rights Fellowship, 179–180

empowerment, 102; personal leadership helping, 145; of team members, 39, 131

enactment, 117, 123, 128–129, 131, 143–144; modes of, 109, *110*, 161–162, *162*; unconscious, 111

ethnographers, 13–14, 25–26

ethnographic study, 15–16, 40, 43

ethnography, 13, 15, 25, 192n2

ethnomethodology, 75

events, 1–2, 3, 109–110

evidence, anecdotal, 23, 135

expectations, 2, 77–79, 143, 173

expenses, 29, 33, 66, 90, 134

factors, for death penalty sentence, 27, 59

facts, 159

failures, 11

Farmer, Millard, 137–138

Fey, Tina, 42

filing, of motions, 70, 134

"finder's keepers" narrative, 154

firefighters, 116–117

first date metaphor, 35–36, 111

food, sending back, 151–152

Fowler, Susan, 72–73, 89–90

framework, for concepts, 160. *See also* cognitive frameworks

Frankl, Viktor, 180

freethinking space, 132

friends, 148–150

fuss, 151–152

"future danger" question, 80, 165

Gandhi, Mahatma, 93
Garcia, Edwardo, 124, 125, 126
generating characters, 121–122
"get outside of yourself" narrative,
    147, 157
ghosting, 111–113
Giddens, Anthony, 192n2
goals, 123, 148–149, 154, 176
"go by" phrase, 35, 49, 57, 121, 174
Graham (defense attorney), 96
Greece, 157–158
Greenhouse, L., 192n2
greenhouse gases, 161
Grisham, John, 181
guards, 185
guided, actions as, 5–6, 7, 48, 56,
    162, 173
guidelines, for death penalty defense
    team, 32–33

Hatch (judge), 94–95, 96, 97,
    164–165
helping friends, 148–150
high performance, 89
history, 4, 27, 58, 60, 122, 129
hitchhikers, 20
Hobson's choice, 73
Holder, Eric, 90, 118, 142
Hollywood, California, 182–183,
    186, 188
the Holocaust, 180
Huffington, Arianna, 118
human resources department,
    72–73
Human Rights and the Corporation
    (MBA course), 180
human rights programs, 179–180

hung juries, 81, 95
hypothesis testing, 120

ID (identification), 185–186
imaginative dreaming, 162, 163
impact, on death penalty, 190
improvisation, 131–132
individual juror questioning (voir
    dire), 81–82, 94, 99–100
induction, 114–115
industry: history, 129; norms, 71,
    134–135
infractions, 166–167
initial public offering (IPO), 178
"innocent unless proven guilty"
    principle, 56
institutional theory, 75, 191n8
institutions, 6, 7, 71, 74–75, 191n8
interactions, social, 48–49
IPO (initial public offering), 178
"irrational loyalty," 177

jail record, of Neely, 166–167
job interviews, 48–49, 128–129
judges, 102–103, 104–105; Hatch,
    94–95, 96, 97, 164–165; written
    rulings from, 66, 67, 68–69
judicial regions, 32
juries, 79–80, 169; hung, 81, 95;
    selection of, 81–82, 94–95, 99, 104
jurors, 169–171; DA coaching, 94–95;
    education of, 99–100
jury deliberations, 100, 139–140,
    164–165; analogies for, 101–102,
    103–104; on Neely, 167–168,
    170–171
justice system, 56, 60, 65, 66, 192n1

Kalanick, Travis, 73–74, 119
Kape, Walter, 24–25, 27, 33–34, 39–41;
    as attorney, 124–125; DA calls,
    136–137
karma, 52
Keefe, Joe, 45–46
Khosrowshahi, Dara, 142–143
knowledge, 2, 25, 34, 117, 128

Lady Justice statues, 61
large-scale transformation, 159,
    174, 190
"launch them into success" narrative,
    176
lawyers. *See* attorneys
leaders, women as, 146, 162–163
"leading the witness," 63
legal rules, 65
legitimacy, 76–77, 89, 129, 144
leisure pool, 75–76
Leon (defendant), 87–88
Lewin, K., 191n1, 193n3
life sentence, 80, 81, 82–83, 95, 125–126
lists, 30–31, 142
logic, 2, 3, 52, 148; blueprint, 4;
    processes, 114
lost wallet, 154–156
Louisiana, 31
Lubbock, Texas, 12, 19, 27, 31, 138

majority rules, 83
male-dominated society, 146
Man's Search for Meaning (Frankl), 180
materials, 119–120
Mead, Margaret, 174
meaning, in suffering, 180

media, social, 111–112, 113
merger, 46, 47, 48
metaphor, first date, 35–36, 111
Mexican restaurants, 55, 74
Mexico, 18
Michelin Tire, 45
middle, in narrative, 122
Midland, Texas, 20
"mini-cap," 136
mistrial, 100, 106
mitigating circumstances, 88, 140
mitigators, 86–87, 107
mock trial, 100
models, 1; narrative change, 51, 71,
    145, 151, 173, 174, 175; personal
    leadership, 145, 146, 159, 175, 190
modes, of enactment, 109, 110,
    161–162, 162
morals, 137
mother, 86; abuse of, 87–88; Neely
    visited by, 22–23
motions: defense, 94; filing of legal,
    70, 134
murder, of Richardson, 21
"murder insurance," 33

narratives: "Can you do it when
    it's hard?," 157, 175; change
    model of, 51, 71, 145, 151, 173, 174,
    175; "conflictioneering," 138;
    construction of, 16, 53, 113–114,
    118; "finder's keepers," 154; "get
    outside of yourself," 147, 157;
    "launch them into success," 176;
    loop of, 50; "reduce spending"
    and "seek justice," 133; "seek

justice," 133; "speak for those who
cannot speak for themselves,"
156, 158; team, 34–35, 41; "the
way things have always been
done," 55, 89, 111, 113–114, 117–118,
128. *See also* "do the right thing"
narrative; *specific topics*
Neely, James, 20–21, 59, 70, 79;
jail record, 166–167; jury
deliberations on, 167–168,
170–171; mother visiting, 22–23;
pretrial hearings, 94, 96, 107;
trial, 90, 164–165
new culture, 8
New York Times, 192n2
New Zealand, 175
norms, 6, 7, 51, 55, 62, 188; of
behavior, 52; cultural, 102;
industry, 71, 134–135; of justice
system, 56, 60, 65, 66; pressures
of, 77, 128, 132; social, 35–36, 37, 38,
74–75; university, 76

objection rules, 63–64
old ways, 5, 6
organizational culture, 13–14, 46–47,
50, 192n1
organizational research, 26, 44
organizational stakeholders, 121–122,
130, 143, 175–176, 179
organizational transformation, 130,
145
organizations, 6, 7, 71, 74–75
origins, of narratives, 37, 53, 120, 132,
146
outcomes, plausible, 123

paleontologists, 115–116
paradigm shift, 89, 115
participant observation, 46
passion (to suffer), 93
patterns, 114–115
Peirce, Charles Sanders, 193n1
"perfect the record," 68, 69, 70,
96–97
personal application, of stakeholder
theory, 149–150
personal leadership model, 145, 146,
159, 175, 190
Peters, T. J., 192n1
phone call, 24
plausible outcomes, 123
plea bargains, 18, 84, 125–126
pollution, 160, 161
positive culture, 40
Powell, W. W., 191nn8–9
practice level, 62, 84, 152
precedent, 97
Prejean, Helen, x
pressures, 1, 52, 62, 71, 73; cultural,
163; of norms, 77, 128, 132
pretrial hearings, Neely, 94, 96, 107
private practice, 30
problem solving, 53–54, 106
pro bono, 41
procedure, appellate, 68, 69
processes, 1, 114; appeals, 64;
construction, 130; logic, 114;
sense-making, 3, 109, 191n4,
193n2
productivity, research, 91
profits, 188
psychology, armchair, 99

public defenders, 84, 85
public services, 84–85

qualitative research, 25
questions: "future danger," 80, 165;
    special issue, 79–80, 82, 140, 165,
    170

race, 59, 60–61
rational assumptions, 84
reality, 1, 36, 48, 184
reality TV shows, 181–182
reconstructive action loops, 77, *78*,
    146, 161
reconstructive behaviors, 78
records: court, 63–64, 65, 69, 98; jail,
    166–167
recreation centers, 75–76
"reduce spending" narrative, 133
refugees, 157–158
relief, 70, 98, 126, 141, 167
report on Uber, Holder, 142
reputation, of Uber, 178
research, 40–41, 83, 104, 188, 189,
    193n4; organizational, 26, 44;
    productivity, 91; qualitative, 25
retrials, 29, 164, 166
Richardson, Ed, 20, 21
rights, 137; constitutional, 31; human,
    179–180; screen, 182, 187–188
risk strategy, 16
Rose, Seth, 18, 56; death penalty for,
    19; trial, 81, 106, 139–141
rules: 10-2 rule, 79, 83, 90, 95, 99, 171;
    legal, 65; majority, 83; objection,
    63–64

rulings, Supreme Court, 96, 97–98
running, 42–43, 47

salient events, 109–110
science, 120, 159
scientific community, 159–160
Scott, W. R., 192n1
screen rights, 182, 187–188
Second City (comedy club), 42, 43,
    44, 45, 49–50
Second City Communications, 42,
    43, 45–46, 46–47
"seek justice" narrative, 133
selection, 109, 132–133, *162*, 163
self-interest, 147
seminar, for defense attorneys, 137
sending back food, 151–152
sense-making processes, 3, 109,
    191n4, 193n2
sentencing hearing, 79, 82, 100, 104
services, social, 175–176
sexual harassment, 72, 73, 118
shareholders, 147–148
skill set "weapons," 153
skits: Clorox narrative, 176–177;
    Second City, 46–47
sobriety, 127, 154
social expectations, 77–79, 173
social interactions, 48–49
social media, 111–112, 113
social norms, 35–36, 37, 38, 74–75
social services, 175–176
social status, 27, 60
society, 37–38, 57, 146
solitary confinement, 167
Sony Pictures studios, 184–186

space, freethinking, 132
"speak for those who cannot speak
    for themselves" narrative, 156, 158
special issue questions, 79–80, 82,
    140, 165, 170
Spencer, Dan, 44
Spielberg, Steven, 181, 183, 184
stakeholders, organizational, 121–122,
    130, 143, 175–176, 179
stakeholder theory, 147–148, 149–150
status, social, 27, 60
stories, 1–2, 4, 26, 39, 43
storytelling, 121–124
strategies, 11, 16, 39, 133, 177
stress, 92
strong culture, 132
structuration theory, 48, 192n2
Subway (fast-food restaurant), 166
success, 3, 8–9
successful trial, 106
to suffer (passion), 93
suffering, meaning in, 180
suicide attempts, 165, 167
Supreme Court, U.S., 58, 60, 61, 70,
    96, 97–98
sustainability, 175
symbolism, 102–103

Task Force for Indigent Defense, 32
taxpayer money, 134, 135
teams: building, 24, 43, 130–132,
    175–176; coordinated, 130–131;
    member empowerment of, 39,
    131; narrative of, 34–35, 41. See also
    death penalty defense team
10–2 rule, 79, 83, 90, 95, 99, 171

tenure, 91, 92, 108, 188
Texas, 29; Code of Criminal
    Procedure, 68; Criminal Defense
    Lawyers Association, 28, 31;
    death sentences in, 16, 17, 58,
    79–80, 83; Lubbock, 12, 19, 27, 31,
    138; Midland, 20; West, 8, 12, 27,
    32, 126
Texas Tech Recreation Center,
    75–76
Texas Tech University, 13, 24, 58, 75,
    91, 180
theories: institutional, 75, 191n8;
    stakeholder, 147–148, 149–150;
    structuration, 48, 192n2
thinking, abductive, 114, 115, 116–117,
    120, 129, 193n1
Thomas, Andy, 19, 141
Toby (defense attorney), 22, 95–96,
    97
traditional breakups, 112
transformation, 6, 8, 10, 98, 119;
    large-scale, 159, 174, 190;
    organizational, 130, 145
trials, 22, 23, 79; bifurcated, 58; mock,
    100; Neely, 90, 164–165; Rose, 81,
    106, 139–141; successful, 106
trust building, 85–86, 88, 129, 132
TV pilot, 187
TV shows, 181–182, 187–188

Uber (ride-sharing company), 9,
    72, 118, 142, 179; "bro culture" of,
    73–74, 90; "do the right thing"
    narrative, 143–144; reputation
    of, 178

unconscious enactment, 111
unconstitutional, death penalty as, 96, 97
underlying assumptions, 129
Unilever, 175
Universal Pictures Studios, 183–184
university norms, 76
unless *vs.* until, 56–57

values, 2, 132; corporate, 175; cultural, 142–143
Van Maanen, J., 192n2
verdicts, 139, 167–168, 169
visions, 1, 4, 5, 39, 98, 189
voices, Garcia hearing, 125
voir dire (individual juror questioning), 81–82, 94, 99–100

waiving, of death penalty, 136
Waterman, R. H., 192n1
"the way things have always been done" narrative, 55, 89, 111, 113–114, 117–118, 128
"weapons," skill set, 153
Weick, Karl, 193n2
West Texas, 8, 12, 27, 32, 126
West Texas Regional Public Defender for Capital Cases, 32
William Morris Agency, 182
windsurfing, 98–99
with (co), 93
women, as leaders, 146, 162–163
workshops, 12, 13, 43, 175–177
written rulings, 66, 67, 68–69, 70
wrong actions, 89